A Year in Earrings

365 Designs and Variations

From the publisher of *BeadStyle* magazine

KALMBACH BOOKS

Kalmbach Books
21027 Crossroads Circle
Waukesha, Wisconsin 53186
www.Kalmbach.com/Books

Published in 2009
13 12 11 10 09   1 2 3 4 5

Manufactured in the United States of America

ISBN: 978-0-87116-296-0

The material in this book has appeared previously in *365 Earrings You Can Make* and *BeadStyle* magazine. *BeadStyle* is registered as a trademark.

Publisher's Cataloging-in-Publication Data

A year in earrings : 365 designs and variations / from the publisher of
  BeadStyle magazine.

        p. : col. ill. ; cm.

   "The material in this book has appeared previously in 365 Earrings You Can Make and BeadStyle magazine."

   ISBN: 978-0-87116-296-0

1. Earrings--Handbooks, manuals, etc. 2. Beadwork--Handbooks, manuals, etc. 3. Jewelry making--Handbooks, manuals, etc. I. Title: Earrings II. Title: BeadStyle Magazine. III. Title: 365 earrings you can make.

TT860 .Y43 2009
745.594/2

Contents

Introduction

You can never have too many earrings.

That's why we've produced *A Year in Earrings: 365 Designs and Variations*. If you need some casual metal earrings that will look great with a pair of jeans, you can find them in Sue Godfrey's "Decorative chain" (p. 69). Need to go more elegant? Anna Elizabeth Draeger's "Dangling coils" (p. 40) add sparkle with their crystals and class with their long, lean design. Or maybe you just want to have fun — check out Monica Han's funky tube-bead stars on p. 54. Whatever you need, we've got you covered. The projects included here use a huge array of materials — crystals, furnace glass, bead caps, spacer bars, chain, wire, lampworked beads, Lucite — so you're sure to find something that will complement whatever you're wearing.

We've added more informative materials to this book as well, supplementing the clear, step-by-step instructions and thorough basic techniques, tools, and materials sections with tips, shortcuts, and suggestions. There's also an explanation of the types of metals best suited for earrings, illustrations and explanations of common types of earring wires, and instructions for making a wide array of your own handcrafted earring findings.

So whether you dig dangles and drops, crave clusters, or have to have hoops, you'll find plenty of earring projects — plus inspiration for creating your own designs — in *A Year in Earrings*. And one thing is for sure — you're going to need a bigger earring tree!

Basics

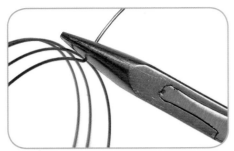

Cutting memory wire

Memory wire is hardened steel, so it will dent and ruin the jaws of most jewelry-grade wire cutters. Use heavy-duty wire cutters or cutters specifically designed for memory wire, or bend the wire back and forth with chainnose pliers until it snaps.

Making a coil

1 Cut a piece of wire to the specified length. Using roundnose pliers, make a loop on one end.
2 Hold the loop with chainnose pliers, and use your fingers to coil the wire around the loop two or three times. Using chainnose pliers, make a right-angle bend in the wire.

Flattened crimp

1 Hold the crimp bead with the tip of your chainnose pliers. Squeeze the pliers firmly to flatten the crimp bead.
2 The flattened crimp. Tug the wire to make sure the crimp has a solid grip. If the wire slides, remove the crimp and repeat the steps with a new crimp bead.

Folded crimp

1 Position the crimp bead in the notch closest to the crimping pliers' handle.
2 Separate the wires and firmly squeeze the crimp bead.
3 Move the crimp bead into the notch at the pliers' tip, and hold the crimp bead. Squeeze the pliers, folding the bead in half at the indentation.
4 The folded crimp. Tug the wire to make sure the crimp has a solid grip. If the wire slides, remove the crimp and repeat the steps with a new crimp bead.

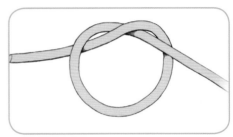

End crimp

1 Glue one end of the cord and place it in a crimp end. Use chainnose pliers to fold one side of the crimp end over the cord.
2 Repeat with the second side of the crimp end and squeeze gently.

Opening a jump ring, earring wire, or loop

1 Hold the jump ring or loop with two pairs of chainnose pliers or with chainnose and roundnose pliers.
2 To open the jump ring or loop, bring one pair of pliers toward you.
3 The open jump ring. Reverse the steps to close.

Overhand knot

Make a loop and pass the working end through it. Pull the ends to tighten the knot.

1

2

1

2

1

2

3

4

3

4

3

4

5

6

Plain loop

1 Trim the wire ⅜ in. (1 cm) above the top bead. Make a right-angle bend close to the bead.
2 Grab the wire's tip with roundnose pliers. Roll the wire to form a half circle. Release the wire.
3 Reposition the pliers in the loop and continue rolling, forming a centered circle above the bead.
4 The finished plain loop.

Wrapped loop

1 Make sure there is at least 1¼ in. (3.2 cm) of wire above the bead. With the tip of your chainnose pliers, grasp the wire directly above the bead. Bend the wire (above the pliers) into a right angle.
2 Position the jaws of your roundnose pliers in the bend.
3 Bring the wire over the top jaw of the pliers. Reposition the pliers' lower jaw snugly in the curved wire.
4 Wrap the wire down and around the bottom of the pliers. This is the "first half of a wrapped loop."
5 Grasp the loop with chainnose pliers.
6 Wrap the wire tail around the stem, covering the stem between the loop and the top bead. Trim the excess wrapping wire and press the end close to the wraps with chainnose or crimping pliers.

Making a set of wraps above a top-drilled bead

1 Center a top-drilled bead on a 3-in. (7.6 cm) piece of wire. Bend each wire upward to form a squared-off U shape.
2 Cross the wires into an X above the bead.
3 Using chainnose pliers, make a small bend in each wire so the ends form a right angle.
4 Wrap the horizontal wire around the vertical wire as in a wrapped loop. Trim the excess wrapping wire.

Tools and materials

Chainnose pliers have smooth, flat inner jaws, and the tips taper to a point. Use them for gripping and for opening and closing loops and jump rings.

Roundnose pliers have smooth, tapered, conical jaws used to make loops. The closer to the tip you work, the smaller the loop will be.

Crimping pliers have two grooves in their jaws that are used to fold or roll a crimp bead into a compact shape.

With **diagonal wire cutters**, use the front of the blades to make a pointed cut and the back of the blades to make a flat cut.

A **mandrel** is used to shape and measure wire, particularly in ring shapes. Some mandrels come printed with ring-size measurements. If you don't want to invest in mandrel, a pen or marker can sometimes serve the same purpose.

A **hammer** is used to harden wire for hoops and bangles. Any hammer with a flat head will work, as long as the head is free of nicks that could mar your metal. The light ball-peen hammer shown here is one of the most commonly used hammers for jewelry making.

A **bench block** or anvil provides a hard, smooth surface on which to hammer your pieces. An anvil is similarly hard but has different surfaces, such as a tapered horn, to help forge wire into different shapes.

Metal files are used to refine and shape the edges of metal and wire surfaces.

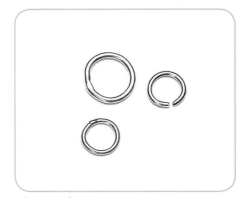

A **jump ring** is used to connect two components. It is a small wire circle or oval that is either open or soldered closed.

Crimp beads are small, large-holed, thin-walled metal beads designed to be flattened or crimped into a tight roll. Use them when stringing jewelry on flexible beading wire.

A **head pin** looks like a blunt, long, thick sewing pin. It has a flat or decorative head on one end to keep beads on. Head pins come in different diameters (or gauges) and lengths.

Flexible beading wire is composed of steel wires twisted together and covered with nylon. This wire is much stronger than thread and does not stretch; the higher the number of inner strands (between three and 49), the more flexible and kink-resistant the wire. It is available in a variety of sizes. Use .014 and .015 for most gemstones, crystals, and glass beads. Use thicker varieties (.018, .019, and .024) for heavy beads or nuggets. Use thinner wire (.010 and .012) for lightweight pieces and beads with very small holes, such as pearls.

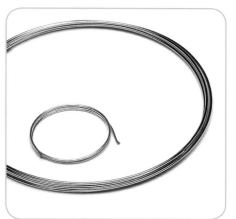

Memory wire is steel spring wire. It comes in several sizes and can be used without clasps to make coiled bracelets, necklaces, and rings.

Wire is available in a number of materials and finishes, including brass, gold, gold-filled, gold-plated, fine silver, sterling silver, anodized niobium (chemically colored wire), and copper. Brass, copper, and craft wire are packaged in 10–40-yd. (9.5–36.6m) spools, while gold, silver, and niobium are usually sold by the foot or ounce. Wire thickness is measured by gauge — the higher the gauge, the thinner the wire — and is available in varying hardnesses and shapes, including twisted, round, half-round, and square.

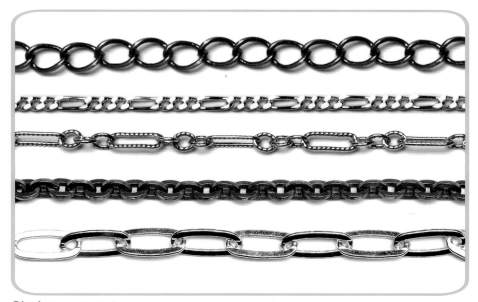

Chain is available in many finishes, including sterling silver and gold-filled as well as base metal or plated metals, and styles, including (from top to bottom) **curb**, **figaro**, **long-and-short**, **rolo**, and **cable**.

Design ideas

The most interesting earring option can be just a spin on traditional beading elements. Try using materials from your other beading projects in unexpected ways — connect them, turn them, rearrange and reimagine them.

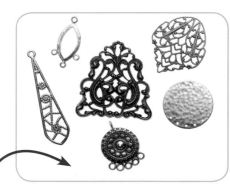

Try accenting an earring wire with a tassel or branch component.

Chandelier components attach to earring findings, offering more loops from which to hang dangles, and can add an elegant or Bohemian flair to your outfit.

Try creating your own chandeliers by connecting filigree components or other findings.

Frame a single bead or a collection of beads in bead frames. Bead frames come in a variety of shapes and styles and could even make attractive earrings when empty.

Stack spacers on top of beads, or wire them together for a long, loopy strand.

Hang dangles from each of the holes of a spacer bar.

Use cones to gather many strands of seed beads or several beads on head pins.

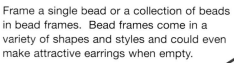

Bead caps can be strung underneath or on top of a single bead, or both.

Use a pinch end clasp to gather fine strands of wire or chain.

Look good coming and going with dangles attached to the front and the back of an earring post.

Dangle textured jump rings from a thin chain.

TYPES OF EARRING WIRES

Your earring wire may be a simple hook to slide through your ears, or it may be an integral part of your earring design.

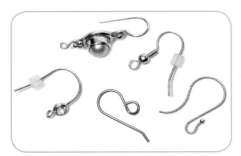

French wires
French wires (also known as fishhooks) often feature a coil or other decorative element on the front. If desired, you can slide a rubber ear nut on the back.

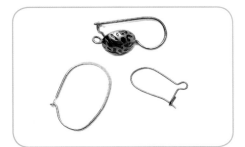

Kidney wires
Kidney wires hook below your ear and around the back of the earring.

Lever-back wires
Lever-back wires hinge open and closed in back.

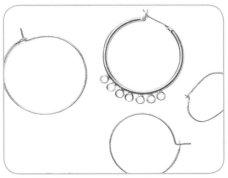

Hoops
Whether a simple hoop or one with loops, hoop findings are great for hanging dangles.

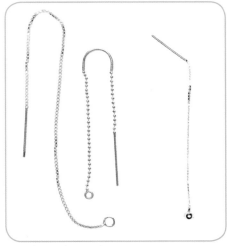

Earring threads
String beads directly onto earring threads or attach dangles to the ends, if they have loops. You can pull the thread halfway through your ear to wear, or weave it through multiple piercings to create loops. Add an ear nut to secure.

Earring posts
Earring posts do not hang below your ear, but they have loops for attaching dangles that do. Earring posts also come in clip-on versions for unpierced ears.

fancy wires

Personalize your designs with unusual earring wires

Check your local bead and craft stores or go online to find unusual wires that add a unique touch or personal flair to your earrings.

hoops with loops

square hoops

graphic designs

gemstone options

MAKING YOUR OWN EARRING WIRES

If you want to challenge yourself, or if you just prefer a DIY aesthetic, try making your own earring wires.

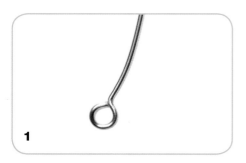
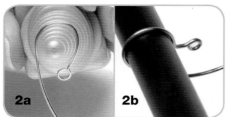

French earring wire (or fishhook)

1 Cut two 2½-in. (6.4 cm) pieces of 20- or 22-gauge half-hard wire. Make a plain loop (Basics) at one end of each.

2 Place the wires side by side on a mandrel **(a)** or around a pen barrel **(b)**. Pull the wires around the mandrel or pen.

3 Trim the excess wire. If you'd like to add texture, hammer the wire on a bench block or anvil now. (If you don't want to texture your earring wires, continue to step 4). Don't hammer too close to the part of the wire that will go through your ear.

4 File the end. Using chainnose pliers, bend the end of each wire upward.

Embellished French earring wire

1 To decorate your earring wires with crystals, spacers, or seed beads, cut a 2-in. (5 cm) piece of 20- or 22-gauge half-hard wire. Make a plain loop (Basics, p. 6). String your selection of decorative beads (this earring wire uses a 4 mm flat spacer and a 4 mm bicone). Make a right-angle bend.

2 Curve the wire around a pen barrel (or mandrel, if you prefer).

3 Using chainnose pliers, bend the end of the wire upward. Trim the excess wire and file the end.

4 On a bench block or anvil, gently hammer the earring wire. Flip the earring wire over and hammer the other side.

Hoop earring wire

1 Cut a piece of 20- or 22-gauge half-hard wire. (The length will depend on how large you want your hoops to be, but you should plan on using ½ in. (1.3 cm) of wire for your plain loop and bent-wire hook to close the hoop.) Wrap the wire around a pen barrel, aspirin bottle, film canister or other round object.

2 If you plan to string your beads directly on the hoop, string them now and center the beads on the wire. If you will attach beads to the hoops as dangles, continue to step 3.

3 Make a plain loop on one end of the wire. Approximately ⅛ in. (3 mm) from the other end, bend the wire up to make a piece that will hook into the plain loop for a closure. File the end.

4 Hammer the hoop on a bench block or anvil, avoiding the loop and bent end **(a)**. If your beads are strung directly on the hoop, slide them to each end to hammer around **(b)**. Be careful not to break the beads. Turn the hoop over and hammer the other side.

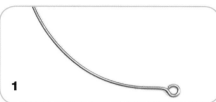

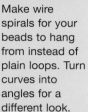

Be creative! Make wire spirals for your beads to hang from instead of plain loops. Turn curves into angles for a different look.

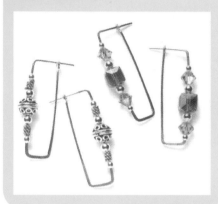

Hooks for findings

1 For hooks that attach to pieces of chain, dangles, or other findings, cut a 2½-in. (6.4 cm) piece of 20- or 22-gauge half-hard wire. Bend the wire so it curves slightly.

2 Make a plain loop (Basics, p. 6) at one end. Using chainnose pliers, bend the loop down so it's at a 45-degree angle from the wire.

3 Open the loop (Basics) on the wire and attach your chain, dangle, or other finding. Close the loop.

Hooks to hold beads

1 For hooks that you can string beads directly onto, cut a 4- to 5-in. (10–13 cm) piece of 20- or 22-gauge half-hard wire. Make a plain loop (Basics, p. 6) on one end.

2 String your beads. At the wire's halfway point, bend it around a pen barrel.

3 To harden the wire, hammer it gently at the bend on a bench block or anvil, carefully avoiding the beads. Turn the wire over and hammer the other side. File the end.

using metals in earrings

Q I just got my ears pierced and want to make some earrings. Can you describe some of the different metals used in earrings?

A Base-metal findings are typically a silver- or gold-colored nickel alloy and are less expensive than other metal findings. One common metal allergy is a sensitivity to nickel. If your ears swell or become itchy, avoid nickel.

Gold-plated metal has a very thin layer of gold on the surface of a base metal. Most commonly, a 10-karat (10k) layer is applied by the process of electroplating. Gold plate is a thinner layer of gold than the amount in a gold-filled finding.

Surgical-grade stainless steel findings are often referred to as "hypoallergenic," but do not equate hypoallergenic with nickel-free. Surgical stainless steel contains a small amount of nickel (usually 8 percent in jewelry). If you are slightly sensitive to nickel, you can probably wear surgical stainless steel for a few hours.

Niobium and titanium can be anodized (coated with oxide) to create colors. Most metal-sensitive people can comfortably wear these lightweight, hypoallergenic metals. Both are soft, and given time, the color will erode to a natural dark gray.

Sterling silver is a combination of pure silver and copper or other alloy. Many nickel-sensitive people can wear sterling silver without experiencing a reaction. In time, sterling silver will take on an antique patina.

Gold-filled wire will last a long time without showing wear. A tube of gold is formed and filled with a base metal, usually jeweler's brass.

The purity or fineness of gold is indicated by its karat number. If you are hypersensitive to nickel alloys, wear 14k (or higher) gold. Fine gold, or 24k gold, is the purest gold for jewelry and is greater than 99.7 percent pure gold.

Great earring tips from other beaders

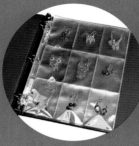

mobile earring display
Sports-card pages are a convenient way to transport and display earrings for sale. Close the top of the packets with double-stick tape to keep the earrings secure while still allowing buyers to remove them for a closer look.
– Nicole Jeske

postcard display
To display earrings, cut postcards and poke two holes in each piece for the earring wires. If you plan to sell the earrings, write the price on the bottom of the card. The price can be cut off if the earrings are given as a gift.
– Ami Coulliard

earring trees
Small artificial trees are a great way to display earrings. They are usually on sale after the holidays. The ones that have fiber-optic branches are especially beautiful.
– Marcy Whiteside

earring display
I display earrings on my business cards. Then, I put them in plastic bags to keep them neat and secure. I tack the bags to a cork board for display on an easel at craft shows. I can fit 50 pairs of earrings on a 15 x 21-in. (38 x 53 cm) board.
– Olivia Wendorf

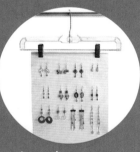

foam ear guards
Use a hole punch and craft foam to make easy, economical ear guards for French earring wires. Make a hole in the center of the foam circle with a sharp pin before putting it on the earring.
– Nicole Jeske

festive packaging
Use plastic Easter eggs or jelly beans as small gift boxes. They're also a great way to transport your jewelry to bead shows and package it for buyers.
– Marcy Whiteside

revolving showcase
Hang pairs of earrings in the holes of an inverted mesh trash can. Put the trash can on a lazy Susan and spin it to see your jewelry at a glance.
– Catie Hoover

at a glance
Attach a piece of needlepoint canvas to the clips on a pant hanger. Hook earrings through the holes in the canvas, and hang the holder in a closet for convenient storage.
– Cindy Klein

Flowing teardrops

They don't call it flexible beading wire for nothing! Paired with an EZ-Crimp, a bit of wire curves gracefully in an amazing number of lightweight earring styles. Use small-diameter beading wire to make sure both ends fit in the crimp. — *Cathy Jakicic*

1

1 Cut a 6-in. (15 cm) piece of beading wire. Center: four 2 mm crystals, 3 mm crystal, 4 mm crystal, 6 mm crystal, 4 mm, 3 mm, four 2 mms.

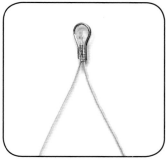

2 String both ends through an EZ-Crimp, tightening the wire until the teardrop is the desired size. Using chainnose pliers, flatten the smooth sides of the EZ-Crimp. Trim the excess wire.

3 Open the loop of an earring wire (Basics, p. 6) and attach the dangle. Close the loop. Make a second earring to match the first.

Supply List

- **2** 6 mm round crystals
- **4** 4 mm bicone crystals
- **4** 3 mm round crystals
- **16** 2 mm round crystals
- flexible beading wire, .015 or thinner
- **2** EZ-Crimps
- pair of earring wires
- chainnose pliers
- diagonal wire cutters

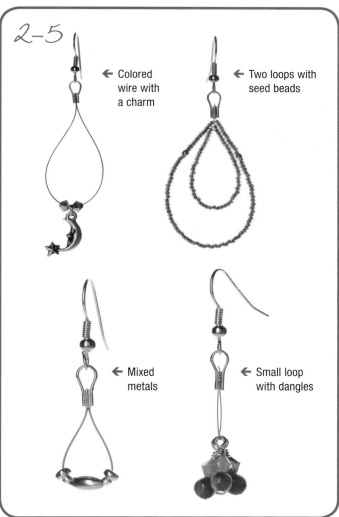

2–5

← Colored wire with a charm

← Two loops with seed beads

← Mixed metals

← Small loop with dangles

Refreshing combinations

The lime and coconut beads I found at the Bead&Button Show gave me the idea for these cocktail earrings. A few simple wrapped loops, and I'm relaxing on a sunny beach. Your personal tastes, the ingredients in your bead pantry, and your thirst for creativity will dictate what you mix up. — *Cathy Jakicic*

6

1 On a head pin, string a bicone crystal, a spacer, and a bicone. Make the first half of a wrapped loop (Basics, p. 6).

On a head pin, string a bicone. Make the first half of a wrapped loop. Make four single-bicone units.

On a head pin, string: round crystal, lime bead, round crystal, spacer, round crystal. Make the first half of a wrapped loop. Make two lime-bead units and two coconut-bead units.

2 Cut a 1½-in. (3.8 cm) piece of chain. Attach a coconut-bead unit and a single-bicone unit to the second or third large link. Skipping a link between each pair, attach the remaining fruit-bead units and single-bicone units, alternating limes and coconuts. Complete the wraps as you go.

Attach the double-bicone unit to the bottom link.

3 Open a 6 mm jump ring (Basics). Attach the dangle and the loop of an earring post. Close the jump ring. Make a second earring to match the first.

Supply List

- **4** 10–15 mm coconut beads (J.P. Imported Beads, jpimported.com)
- **4** 10–15 mm lime beads (J.P. Imported Beads)
- **12** 5 mm bicone crystals
- **24** 2 mm round crystals
- **10** 3 mm flat spacers
- 3 in. (7.6 cm) figure-eight chain, 2 mm links
- **18** 1½-in. (3.8 cm) head pins
- **2** 6 mm jump rings
- pair of earring posts with ear nuts
- chainnose pliers
- roundnose pliers
- diagonal wire cutters

7-11

← Rum and coke: topaz crystals with a splash of copper

← Seltzer with lime: crystal with a twist of light olivine

← Strawberry shake: rose and white pearls with rose crystals

← Coffee with cream: jet crystals and striped jasper on a robust chain

← Tequila sunrise: bicones in golds and orange

Changing dangles

The best part of these simple hoops is that with large enough wrapped loops, you can create a wardrobe of earrings with the same basic finding. There is no end to what these circles can do, so get rolling.

— *Julie D'Amico-Beres*

12

13–15

← With a chain dangle

← With chain loops

← Single art bead (Lisa Kan, lisakan.com)

1 On a head pin, string: bicone crystal, bead cap, Venetian-glass bead, bead cap, bicone. Make a wrapped loop (Basics, p. 6) with the largest part of your roundnose pliers.

2 Open the hinge on a hoop earring and attach the dangle. Make a second earring to match the first.

Supply List

- **2** 15 mm round Venetian-glass beads
- **4** 4 mm bicone crystals
- **4** 4–6 mm bead caps
- **2** 2-in. (5 cm) head pins
- pair of hinged hoop earrings
- chainnose pliers
- roundnose pliers
- diagonal wire cutters

No-fuss finery

There's nothing fussy about creating these chandelier earrings. Just hang chain, WireLace, dangles, or a combination of materials. Better yet, explore your own bright ideas. — *Cathy Jakicic*

16

1 On a head pin, string a round bead. Make the first half of a wrapped loop (Basics, p. 6). Make a total of four round-bead units. Repeat to make an oval-bead unit.

2 Cut five 1-in. (2.5 cm) pieces of chain. Attach a bead unit to each chain. Complete the wraps.

Supply List

- **2** 6 mm oval beads
- **8** 3 mm round beads
- **2** five-loop chandelier findings
- 11 in. (28 cm) cable chain, 1.5–2 mm links
- **10** 1½-in. (3.8 cm) head pins
- **10** 4 mm jump rings
- pair of earring wires
- chainnose pliers
- roundnose pliers
- diagonal wire cutters

3 **a** Open a jump ring (Basics). Attach the oval-bead dangle and the center loop of a chandelier finding. Close the jump ring.

b Use jump rings to attach the round-bead dangles and the remaining loops. Open the loop of an earring wire (Basics) and attach the chandelier finding. Close the loop. Make a second earring to match the first.

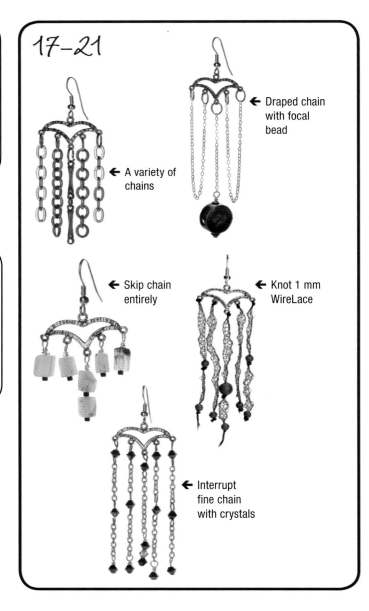

17–21

← Draped chain with focal bead

← A variety of chains

← Skip chain entirely

← Knot 1 mm WireLace

← Interrupt fine chain with crystals

Spacer bars

Weave beading wire through the holes of a long spacer bar for a modern look. Change the weave, the number of bars, or the beads you use to explore the spacer bar's vast style frontier. — *Cathy Jakicic*

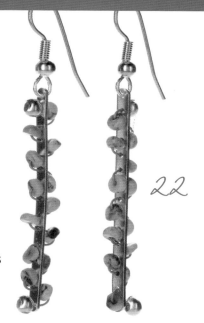

22

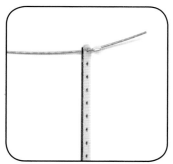

1 Cut a 6-in. (15 cm) piece of beading wire. String the first hole of a spacer bar and a crimp bead. Flatten the crimp bead (Basics, p. 6).

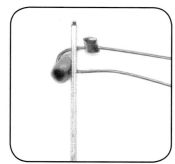

2 String a rondelle and the next hole of the spacer bar.

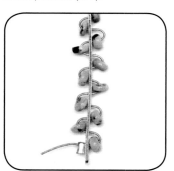

3 Repeat step 2 until the wire is strung through the second-to-last hole of the spacer bar. String a crimp bead and tighten the wire. Flatten the crimp bead. Trim the excess wire.

4 a With chainnose pliers, gently close a crimp cover over each crimp bead.
b Open the loop of an earring wire (Basics). Attach the dangle and close the loop. Make a second earring to match the first.

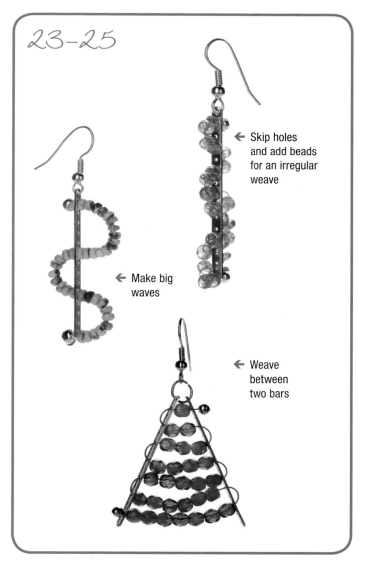

23-25

← Skip holes and add beads for an irregular weave

← Make big waves

← Weave between two bars

Lean drops

Long, lean beads make natural dangles all by themselves. You can create spare or lush earrings — with straight or curved profiles — in a variety of vertical combinations. — *Cathy Jakicic*

26

1 Open a jump ring (Basics, p. 6). Attach a wood paddle bead. Close the jump ring.

2 Use a jump ring to attach a paddle, the first jump ring, and a paddle.

3 Open the loop of an earring wire (Basics). Attach the dangle and close the loop. Make a second earring to match the first.

Supply List

- **6** 26 mm wood paddle beads
- **4** 6 mm jump rings
- pair of earring wires
- chainnose and roundnose pliers, or **2** pairs of chainnose pliers

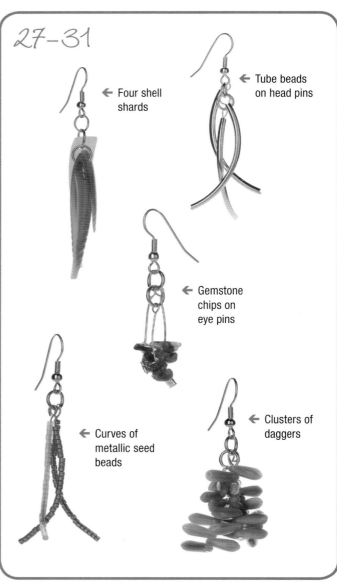

27-31

← Four shell shards

← Tube beads on head pins

← Gemstone chips on eye pins

← Curves of metallic seed beads

← Clusters of daggers

Furnace glass

Slices of furnace glass with candy-colored stripes make cheery, whimsical earrings. Their geometric shapes give tons of options for contemporary designs. My favorite: a stack of colors bracketed with bold crystals. — *Naomi Fujimoto.*

1 On a head pin, string a bicone crystal, three furnace-glass beads, and a cone crystal. Make a wrapped loop (Basics, p. 6).

2 Open the loop of an earring wire (Basics). Attach the dangle and close the loop. Make a second earring to match the first.

Supply List

- **6** 10–15 mm furnace-glass beads, **2** each in three styles
- **2** 8 mm bicone crystals
- **2** 6.6 mm cone crystals
- **2** 2-in. (5 cm) 22-gauge head pins

- pair of earring wires
- chainnose pliers
- roundnose pliers
- diagonal wire cutters

33-38

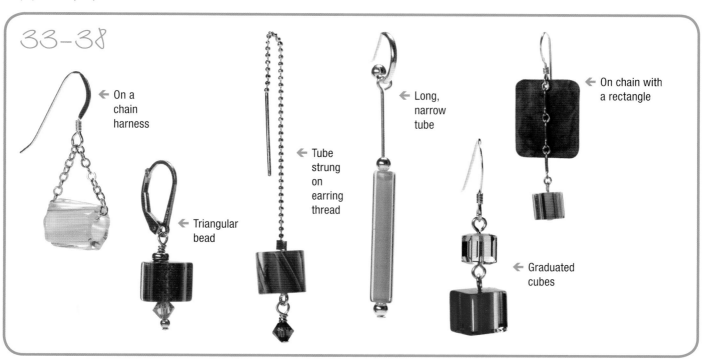

← On a chain harness

← Triangular bead

← Tube strung on earring thread

← Long, narrow tube

← On chain with a rectangle

← Graduated cubes

Sweet hearts

Nothing says, "It's Valentine's Day," like these darling little heart beads. The flat heart-shaped beads are available in several color mixes. If your love is large, be bold and try bigger hearts. — *Jane Konkel*

39

1a Lay out the beads on your work space, balancing colors.
b Cut a 2½-in. (6.4 cm) piece of wire. On one end, using the largest part of your roundnose pliers, make the first half of a wrapped loop (Basics, p. 6). Attach a heart bead and complete the wraps.

2a String a round spacer and a bicone crystal. Make the first half of a wrapped loop.
b Repeat step 1b and 2a to make a second single-bicone unit, two two-bicone units, and one three-bicone unit. Attach a single-bicone unit to an outer loop of a chandelier finding, and complete the wraps.

Supply List

Ceramic beads from Embroidered Soul, embroideredsoul.com.

- **10** 10 mm heart-shaped ceramic beads, in five colors
- **2** 6 mm round ceramic beads
- **20** 4 mm bicone crystals, in five colors
- **22** 3 mm round spacers
- 30 in. (76 cm) 24-gauge half-hard wire

- **2** 1½-in. (3.8 cm) head pins
- pair of heart-shaped chandelier findings
- pair of lever-back earring wires
- chainnose pliers
- roundnose pliers
- diagonal wire cutters

3 Attach the remaining bead units as shown, completing the wraps as you go.

4 On a head pin, string a spacer and a bicone. Make a plain loop (Basics). Open the loop (Basics) and attach the bead unit to the chandelier finding's inner loop. Close the loop.

5 Cut a 2½-in. (6.4 cm) piece of wire. On one end, make the first half of a wrapped loop. Attach the chandelier finding's top loop; complete the wraps. String a 6 mm bead and a spacer. Make a wrapped loop.

6 Open the loop of an earring wire (Basics). Attach the dangle and close the loop. Make a second earring to match the first.

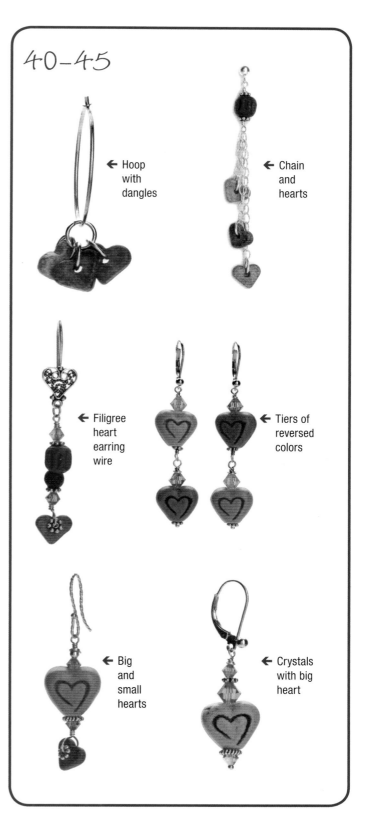

40–45

← Hoop with dangles

← Chain and hearts

← Filigree heart earring wire

← Tiers of reversed colors

← Big and small hearts

← Crystals with big heart

Groovy pendulums

Get in the swing of things with a pair of playful earrings. Like miniature pinwheels, the disk beads spin in the wind. Swirled art beads are ideal for this design. — *Heather Powers*

46

1 Cut a 4-in. (10 cm) piece of wire. Make a right-angle bend in the center. String a spacer, a disk bead, and a spacer.

2 Bend the wire around the spacers.

3 Make a set of wraps (Basics, p. 6) ½ in. (1.3 cm) from the ends of the wire. Make a plain loop (Basics) above the wraps.

4 Open the loop of an earring wire (Basics). Attach the dangle and close the loop. Make a second earring to match the first.

Supply List

- **2** 14 mm disk beads
- **4** 3–4 mm spacers
- **8** in. (20 cm) 24-gauge half-hard wire
- pair of earring wires
- chainnose pliers
- roundnose pliers
- diagonal wire cutters

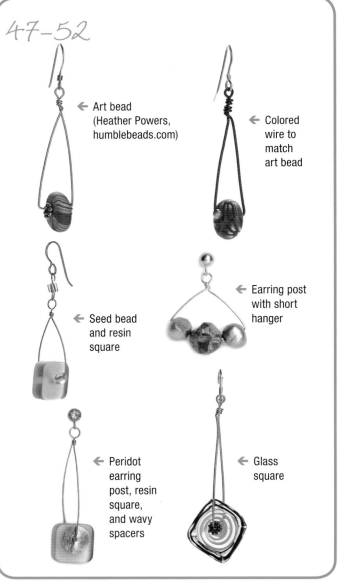

47-52

← Art bead (Heather Powers, humblebeads.com)

← Colored wire to match art bead

← Seed bead and resin square

← Earring post with short hanger

← Peridot earring post, resin square, and wavy spacers

← Glass square

Bold
hexagons

Check out these brightly colored hexagon beads —
both the shape and the contrasting colors pair brilliantly.
Embellish them with chain or crystal-studded links,
or stack 'em like mini stone pavers. — *Jane Konkel*

53

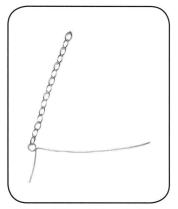

1 Cut a 2½-in. (6.4 cm) piece of wire. Make the first half of a wrapped loop (Basics, p. 6) on one end. Cut a 3-in. (7.6 cm) piece of chain. Attach the loop to one end of the chain, and complete the wraps.

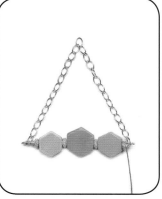

2 String an alternating pattern of four spacers and three hexagon beads. Make the first half of a wrapped loop. Attach the loop to the remaining end link and complete the wraps.

3 Open the loop of an earring wire (Basics). Attach the chain's center link and close the loop. Make a second earring to match the first.

Supply List

- **6** 9–10 mm hexagon beads, **2** in one color, **4** in another (The Earth Bazaar, theearthbazaar.com)
- **8** 3 mm spacers
- 5 in. (13 cm) 24-gauge half-hard wire
- 6 in. (15 cm) chain, 2 mm links
- pair of lever-back earring wires
- chainnose pliers
- roundnose pliers
- diagonal wire cutters

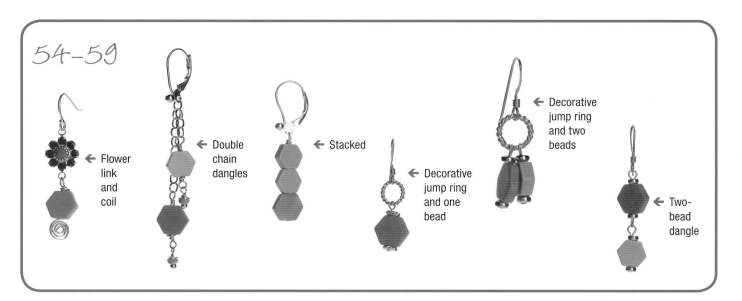

54-59

← Flower link and coil

← Double chain dangles

← Stacked

← Decorative jump ring and one bead

← Decorative jump ring and two beads

← Two-bead dangle

Love these links

Shapely links are a lightweight frame for beads. This pair shows off twisted-oval beads that mimic the slender marquise-shaped links. Connect single links to form some not-so-hooplike hoops. Or, leave out the bead for links and links of fun. — *Jane Konkel*

60

1 On a head pin, string a twisted oval bead. Using the largest part of your roundnose pliers, make the first half of a wrapped loop (Basics, p. 6).

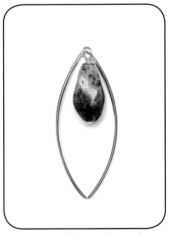

2 Attach a link and complete the wraps.

3 Open a jump ring (Basics), and attach the dangle and the loop of an earring wire. Close the loop. Make a second earring to match the first.

Supply List

Links from Rings & Things, rings-things.com.

- **2** 21 mm metal links
- **2** 15 mm twisted-oval beads
- **2** 1½-in. (3.8 cm) head pins
- **2** 4–5 mm jump rings
- pair of lever-back earring wires
- chainnose pliers
- roundnose pliers
- diagonal wire cutters

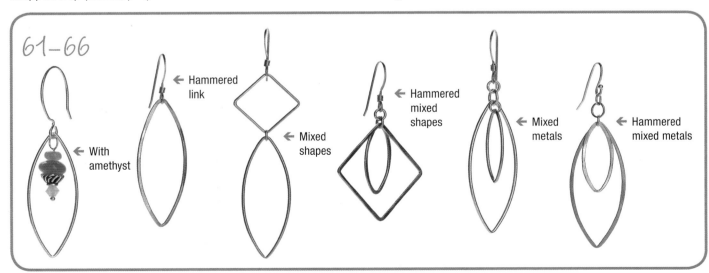

61–66

← With amethyst

← Hammered link

← Mixed shapes

← Hammered mixed shapes

← Mixed metals

← Hammered mixed metals

Chain tassels

Premade tassels offer endless possibilities for making quick, simple earrings. You can embellish the ends with metal beads, or incorporate crystals or a single focal bead in the middle of the tassel. You can even decorate the tassel's bullet end with flat-back crystals. For a more understated look, leave the tassels plain or trim the chains short before you attach beads. Tassels are sold by the dozen and are available in a variety of finishes and chain styles, so go ahead and try several variations. — *Lindsay Mikulsky*

67

1 On a head pin, string an accent bead and make the first half of a wrapped loop (Basics, p. 6). Make eight bead units.

2 On a tassel, attach a bead unit to the end of each chain. Complete the wraps.

3 Open the loop of an earring wire (Basics) and attach the tassel. Close the loop. Make a second earring to match the first.

Supply List

- **2** 1½-in. (3.8 cm) eight-strand chain tassels (Rings & Things, rings-things.com)
- **16** 4–6 mm metal accent beads, in two or three styles
- **16** 1½-in. (3.8 cm) 24-gauge head pins
- pair of earring wires
- chainnose pliers
- roundnose pliers
- diagonal wire cutters

68–73

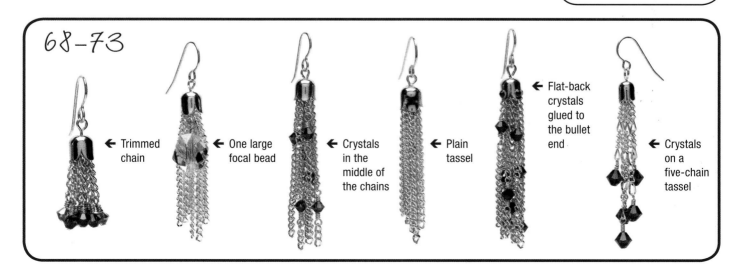

← Trimmed chain

← One large focal bead

← Crystals in the middle of the chains

← Plain tassel

← Flat-back crystals glued to the bullet end

← Crystals on a five-chain tassel

Keshi pearls

Keshi pearls are a classy starting point for multiple pairs of earrings. Whether you attach them to chain, stack them on head pins, or bunch them together, the look is elegant. Try pairing them with silk-colored crystals. — *Lindsay Mikulsky*

74

1 On a head pin, string a keshi pearl. Make the first half of a wrapped loop (Basics, p. 6). Make seven pearl units.

2 Cut a piece of chain with seven large links. Attach a pearl unit to each large link, alternating each side of the chain. Complete the wraps as you go.

3 Open the loop of an earring wire (Basics). Attach the dangle and close the loop. Make a second earring to match the first.

Supply List

- **14** 6–8 mm keshi pearls, center drilled
- 2–3 in. (5–7.6 cm) figure-eight chain, 2–3 mm links (The Earth Bazaar, theearthbazaar.com)
- **14** 1½-in. (3.8 cm) 24-gauge head pins
- pair of earring wires
- chainnose pliers
- roundnose pliers
- diagonal wire cutters

75-78

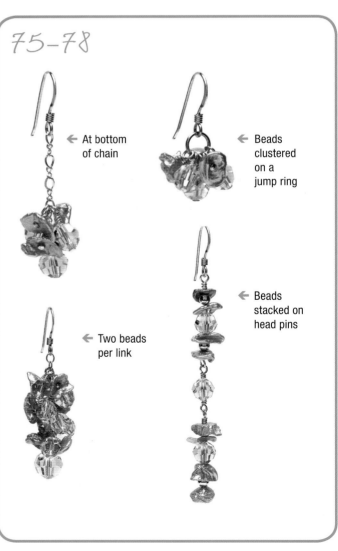

← At bottom of chain

← Beads clustered on a jump ring

← Two beads per link

← Beads stacked on head pins

Cosmic rings

CRYSTALLIZED™ Swarovski Elements cosmic rings add instant dazzle to any design. They're available in three sizes and in a variety of colors. Consider attaching small rings to earring threads, or if you like a bolder look, use large rings embellished with crystal drops. You can even mix up your designs by adding crystal squares. — *Lindsay Mikulsky*

79

1 Open a 9 mm jump ring (Basics, p. 6). Attach two cosmic rings. Close the jump ring. Use a 9 mm jump ring to attach one cosmic ring to a third cosmic ring. Attach a third 9 mm jump ring to the top cosmic ring.

2 Use a 4 mm jump ring to attach the dangle and the loop of an earring wire. Make a second earring to match the first.

Supply List

All components from Fusion Beads, fusionbeads.com.

- **6** 14 mm cosmic rings
- **6** 9 mm jump rings
- **2** 4 mm jump rings
- pair of earring wires
- chainnose and roundnose pliers, or **2** pairs of chainnose pliers

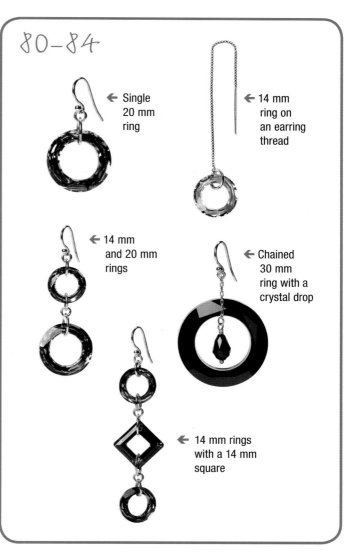

80-84

← Single 20 mm ring

← 14 mm ring on an earring thread

← 14 mm and 20 mm rings

← Chained 30 mm ring with a crystal drop

← 14 mm rings with a 14 mm square

Twisted-wire coils

Twisted-wire coils make charming embellishments for earrings. Make short earrings for a casual look or link coils for long, eye-catching dangles. The single-pearl dangles even look great on hoop earrings. Or, try making your coils out of plain wire and then hammering them for texture. — *Alice Lauber*

85

1 Cut a 3–4-in. (7.6–10 cm) piece of twisted wire. Using roundnose pliers, make a coil. Trim the wire, leaving a ½-in. (1.3 cm) tail. Bend the wire perpendicular to the coil, and make a plain loop (Basics, p. 6).

2 Cut a 2-in. (5 cm) piece of 24-gauge wire. Make a plain loop on one end. Open the loop (Basics) and attach the coil. Close the loop. On the wire, string a spacer, a pearl, and a spacer. Make a wrapped loop (Basics) perpendicular to the plain loop.

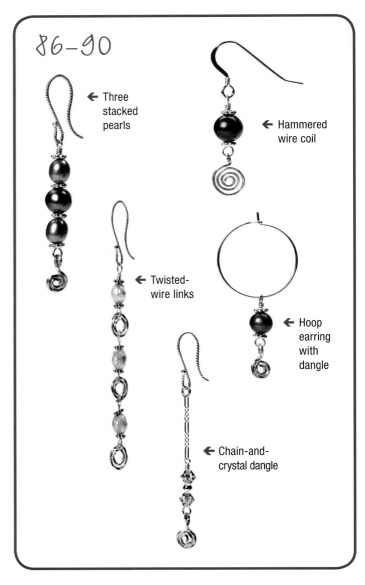

86–90

← Three stacked pearls

← Hammered wire coil

← Twisted-wire links

← Hoop earring with dangle

← Chain-and-crystal dangle

3 Open the loop of an earring wire (Basics) and attach the dangle. Close the loop. Make a second earring in the mirror image of the first.

Supply List

- **2** 6–10 mm pearls
- **4** 3–4 mm flat spacers
- 6–8 in. (15–20 cm) 20- or 22-gauge twisted wire (Midwest Beads, midwestbeads.com)
- 4 in. (10 cm) 24-gauge half-hard wire
- pair of earring wires
- chainnose pliers
- roundnose pliers
- diagonal wire cutters

Vermeil disks

Textured vermeil disks are fun and a little futuristic, but their golden glow is also warm and sophisticated. Stack them on head pins, connect them as bead units, or suspend them from chain. A monochromatic color scheme works well with these designs, or you can add tiny sparks of color with pastel or berry-colored crystals. — *Lindsay Mikulsky*

91

1 Cut three pieces of chain: ½ in., 1 in., and 1½ in. (1.3 cm, 2.5 cm, and 3.8 cm). Cut a 4-in. (10 cm) piece of wire. On one end, make the first half of a wrapped loop (Basics, p. 6). Attach the chains and complete the wraps.

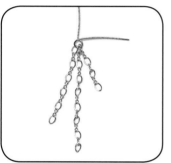

2 On the wire, string: rondelle, disk bead, rondelle, disk, rondelle, disk, rondelle. Make a wrapped loop.

3 Open the loop of an earring wire (Basics). Attach the dangle and close the loop. Make a second earring in the mirror image of the first.

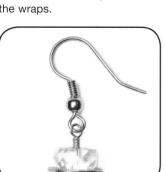

Supply List

- **6** 10 mm vermeil disk beads (The Earth Bazaar, theearthbazaar.com)
- **8** 8 mm faceted rondelles
- **8** in. (20 cm) 22- or 24-gauge half-hard wire
- **6** in. (15 cm) figure-8 chain, 2–3 mm links (The Earth Bazaar)
- pair of earring wires
- chainnose pliers
- roundnose pliers
- diagonal wire cutters

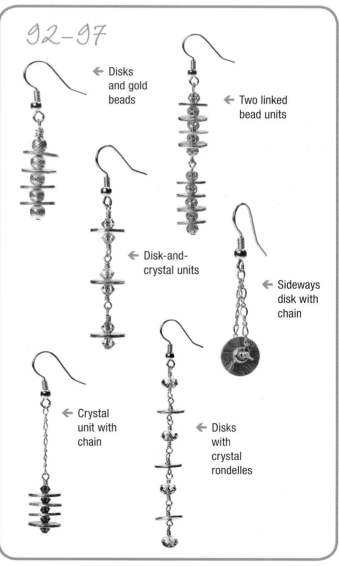

92–97

← Disks and gold beads

← Two linked bead units

← Disk-and-crystal units

← Sideways disk with chain

← Crystal unit with chain

← Disks with crystal rondelles

Pearl clusters

Ingenious use of long-and-short–link chain is the basis for these dressy earrings: the clusters form when you string pairs of beads through the short links. Attach the chain and the earring wire first. It's easier to pick up the earring wire, rather than the chain, as you're attaching the pearls. — *Salena Safranski*

98

1 Cut a piece of chain that has two long links. Open the loop of an earring wire (Basics, p. 6). Attach the chain and close the loop.

2 Cut a ¾-in. (1.9 cm) piece of wire. Using roundnose pliers, make a tiny loop at one end. Flatten the loop with chainnose pliers.

3 On the wire, string a pearl, a short chain link, and a pearl. Make a flattened loop next to the pearl.

4 Repeat steps 2 and 3 with the remaining short links. The middle pair of pearls will be perpendicular to the other pairs.

Supply List

- **2** 6–9 mm glass beads
- **12** 3–4 mm round pearls
- 2–2½ in. (5–6.4 cm) chain, one-long-and-three-short link, 6–8 mm
- 8½ in. (21.6 cm) 24-gauge half-hard wire
- pair of earring wires
- chainnose pliers
- roundnose pliers
- diagonal wire cutters

5 Cut a 2-in. (5 cm) piece of wire. Make a small loop on one end. Make a coil around the loop (Basics).

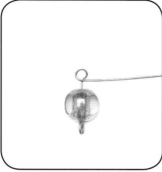

6 String a glass bead and make the first half of a wrapped loop (Basics) perpendicular to the coil.

7 Attach the bead unit to the bottom chain link. Complete the wraps. Make a second earring to match the first.

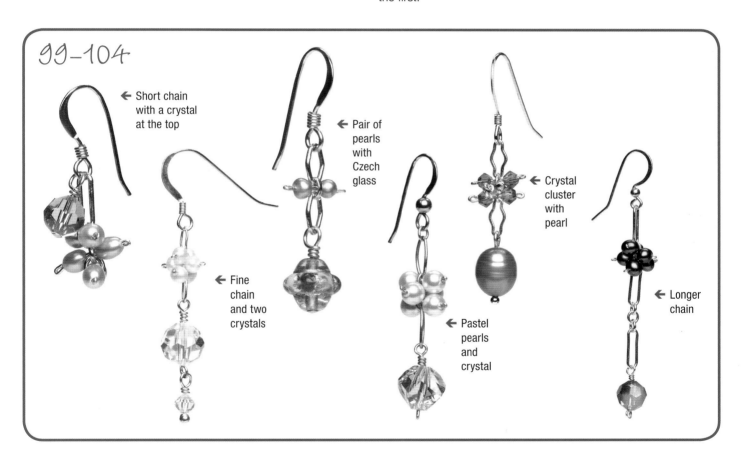

99–104

← Short chain with a crystal at the top

← Pair of pearls with Czech glass

← Fine chain and two crystals

← Crystal cluster with pearl

← Pastel pearls and crystal

← Longer chain

Mix and match

The secret to these mismatched earrings? In each pair, only one element is different — whether it's the color, the theme, or the shape of the dangles. If your style is conservative, you can make the change a subtle one, but make each earring about the same length. — *Monica Han*

105

1 Cut a 2-in. (5 cm) piece of wire. Make the first half of a wrapped loop (Basics, p. 6) on one end. Attach one loop of a flower component and complete the wraps.

2 String a 6 mm bead and make a wrapped loop perpendicular to the first loop.

3 Open the loop of an earring wire (Basics). Attach the dangle and close the loop. Make a second earring to complement the first.

Supply List

- **2** 9 mm flower components, in two colors (Rings & Things, rings-things.com)
- **2** 6 mm round beads
- 4 in. (10 cm) 24-gauge half-hard wire
- pair of earring wires
- chainnose pliers
- roundnose pliers
- diagonal wire cutters

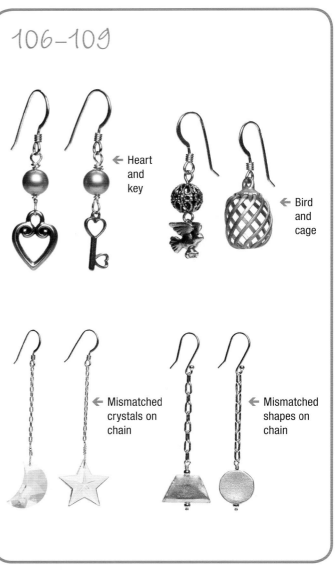

106–109

← Heart and key

← Bird and cage

← Mismatched crystals on chain

← Mismatched shapes on chain

Wired disks

Harness disk beads with a simple wire wrap that's an integral part of the design. Use either 24- or 26-gauge wire, depending on how prominent you want the wraps to be. Use chainnose pliers to hold the loop closed, and wrap the wire with your fingers — it's easier than maneuvering with pliers. — *Heather Boardman*

110

1 Cut an 8-in. (20 cm) piece of wire. Bend it in half to make a loop. String both ends through a disk bead, bending the wire up. Leave about ¼ in. (6 mm) of the loop extending beyond the bead.

2 Wrap each end around the loop's stem in opposite directions.

3 Continue wrapping each end around the stem, leaving the loop open. Trim the excess wire and use chainnose pliers to tuck the ends.

4 Open the loop of an earring wire (Basics, p. 6). Attach the dangle and close the loop. Make a second earring to match the first.

111–114

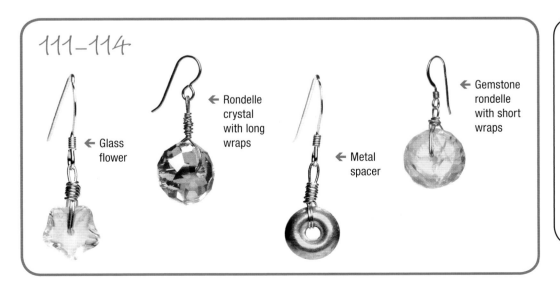

← Glass flower

← Rondelle crystal with long wraps

← Metal spacer

← Gemstone rondelle with short wraps

Supply List

- **2** disk-shaped beads, approximately 15 mm (glass beads from Heather Boardman, hmbstudios.com)
- 16 in. (41 cm) 24- or 26-gauge half-hard wire
- pair of earring wires
- chainnose and roundnose pliers, or **2** pairs of chainnose pliers
- diagonal wire cutters

Textured metal rings

To maximize your design options, buy metal rings both with and without holes. The rings lend themselves to contemporary designs, and you can give them an organic or classic spin by incorporating cord or crystals. Experiment with round or oval jump rings, too. — *Naomi Fujimoto*

115

1 On a head pin, string a crystal. Make a plain loop (Basics, p. 6).

2 Open the loop and attach the bead unit to a hole in a large metal ring. Close the loop. Open a jump ring (Basics), and attach the remaining hole of the large ring and one hole of a small ring. Close the jump ring.

3 Open the loop of an earring wire (Basics). Attach the remaining hole of the dangle and close the loop. Make a second earring to match the first.

Supply List

Metal rings from Nina Designs, ninadesigns.com.

- **2** 21 mm metal rings
- **2** 15 mm metal rings
- **2** 8 mm crystals
- **2** 1½-in. (3.8 cm) head pins
- **2** 4–5 mm jump rings
- pair of earring wires
- chainnose pliers
- roundnose pliers
- diagonal wire cutters

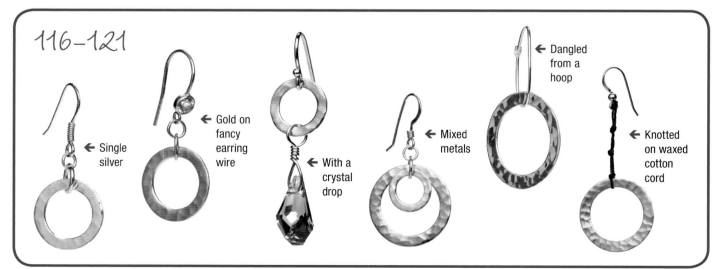

116-121

← Single silver

← Gold on fancy earring wire

← With a crystal drop

← Mixed metals

← Dangled from a hoop

← Knotted on waxed cotton cord

Tibetan beads

If you want to go organic, handmade-bead earrings will suit your style every day of the week. The size and detail of these finely wrought beads benefit from the simplest of settings. Here, brass beads inlaid with gemstones are flanked by turquoise rondelles.

— *Naomi Fujimoto*

122

1 On a head pin, string: spacer, rondelle, focal bead, rondelle, spacer. Make a plain loop (Basics, p. 6).

2 Open the loop of an earring wire (Basics). Attach the bead unit and close the loop. Make a second earring to match the first.

Supply List

All focal beads from Kipuka Trading, kipukatrading.com.

- **2** 10–35 mm focal beads
- **4** 4–6 mm turquoise rondelles

- **4** 3–5 mm spacers
- **2** 2-in. (5 cm) head pins
- pair of earring wires
- chainnose pliers
- roundnose pliers
- diagonal wire cutters

123-127

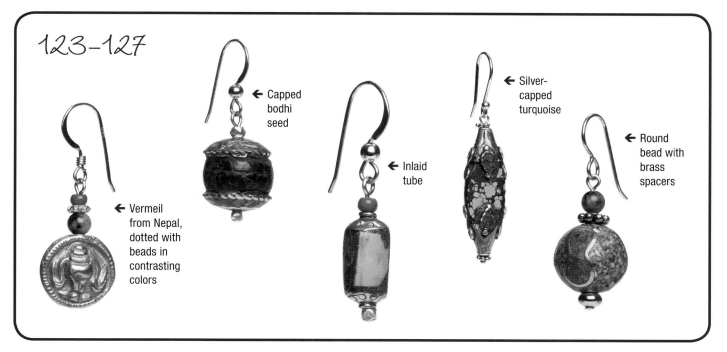

← Vermeil from Nepal, dotted with beads in contrasting colors

← Capped bodhi seed

← Inlaid tube

← Silver-capped turquoise

← Round bead with brass spacers

Double-drilled nuggets

Double-drilled beads offer new options and a few challenges. It helps to remember that, depending on the design, stringing through the second hole is an opportunity, not an obligation. Try aligning the beads horizontally or vertically to take your style in different directions. — *Cathy Jakicic*

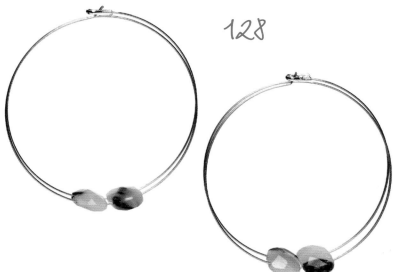

128

Supply List

- **4** 15 mm faceted nugget beads, double drilled (Dakota Stones, dakotastones.com)
- 2½-in. (6.4 cm)-diameter memory wire
- **2** EZ-Crimp findings
- chainnose pliers
- heavy-duty wire cutters (optional)
- G-S Hypo Cement
- metal file or emery board

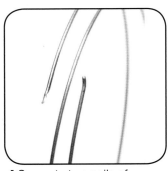

1 Separate two coils of memory wire and cut (Basics, p. 6).

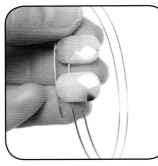

2 String two beads to the center of the wire.

3 String the second set of holes on one wire end. Center the beads.

4 Put a dot of glue on one end of the wire. String an EZ-Crimp. With chainnose pliers, flatten the smooth sides of the EZ-Crimp.

5 With chainnose pliers, bend ¼ in. (6 mm) of the wire at the other end at a 45-degree angle. File the end. Make a second earring to match the first.

129-134

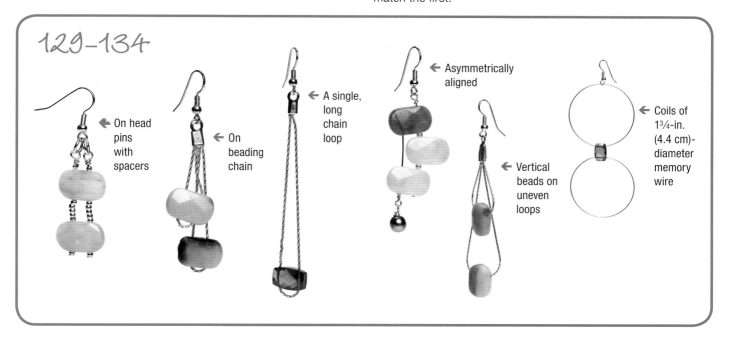

← On head pins with spacers

← On beading chain

← A single, long chain loop

← Asymmetrically aligned

← Vertical beads on uneven loops

← Coils of 1¾-in. (4.4 cm)-diameter memory wire

Dangling coils

Coiling head pins is a pretty way to link crystals and chain. Mix things up with colored Artistic Wire or a rainbow's variety of crystals. — *Anna Elizabeth Draeger*

1 Cut a 1-in. (2.5 cm) piece of wire. Center a bicone crystal on the wire. Make a plain loop (Basics, p. 6) on each end.

On a head pin, string a bicone. Make a plain loop. Make nine head-pin units.

2 On a head pin, string a bicone. Wrap the wire around your roundnose pliers, leaving ¼ in. (6 mm) at the end of the head pin. Make 14 coiled units.

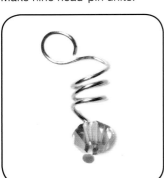

3 Make a plain loop at the end of each coiled unit.

135

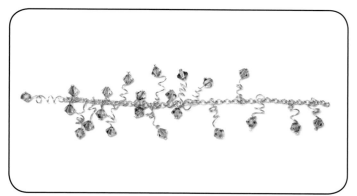

Supply List

- **48** 4 mm bicone crystals
- 2 in. (5 cm) 24-gauge half-hard wire
- 7 in. (18 cm) rolo chain, 2 mm links
- **46** 2-in. (5 cm) head pins
- pair of earring wires
- chainnose pliers
- roundnose pliers
- diagonal wire cutters

4 Cut a 3½-in. (8.9 cm) piece of chain. Open a loop on one coiled unit. Attach the unit to one end of the chain and close the loop. Attach the remaining coiled and head-pin units to the chain.

5 Open each loop of the two-loop unit. Attach an earring wire and the dangle and close the loops. Make a second earring to match the first.

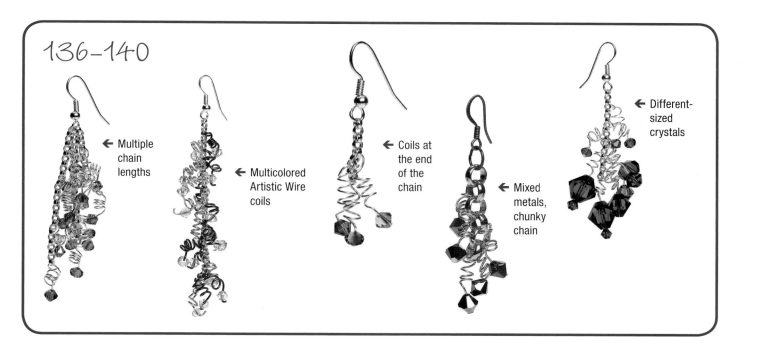

136–140

← Multiple chain lengths

← Multicolored Artistic Wire coils

← Coils at the end of the chain

← Mixed metals, chunky chain

← Different-sized crystals

Simply gems

When you have a spectacularly cut gemstone bead, the best approach is to simply let its beauty shine through. Simplicity doesn't mean you have no options, though. There are a number of ways to subtly enhance a stone. — *Cathy Jakicic*

141

1 Cut a 4-in. (10 cm) piece of 26-gauge wire. String a nugget bead and make a set of wraps above it (Basics, p. 6). Make a wrapped loop (Basics).

2 Cut a 4-in. (10 cm) piece of 24-gauge wire. With chainnose pliers, make a small hook on one end. Wrap the wire horizontally around the nugget, and loop the wire around the hook.

3 Wrap the wire around the nugget twice. String the end through the loop formed in step 2. Make a small bend in the wire and trim the excess. Use roundnose pliers to twist the bend (to tighten the wraps) if necessary.

4 Open the loop of an earring wire (Basics) and attach the dangle. Close the loop. Make a second earring to match the first.

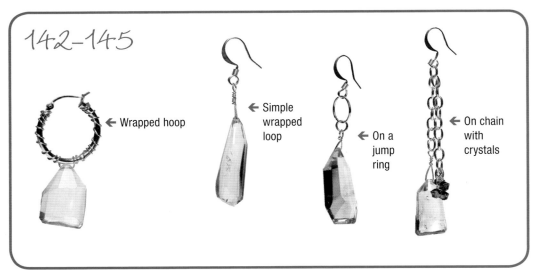

142-145

← Wrapped hoop

← Simple wrapped loop

← On a jump ring

← On chain with crystals

Supply List

- **2** 22–26 mm faceted nugget beads, top drilled
- 8 in. (20 cm) 24-gauge half-hard wire
- 8 in. (20 cm) 26-gauge half-hard wire
- pair of earring wires
- chainnose pliers
- roundnose pliers
- diagonal wire cutters

Sparkling circles

The symmetry of a perfect circle can be the basis for classic, creative designs. By simply rearranging these components, you can create a number of great looks without reinventing the wheel. — *Melinda Jernigan*

146

1 On a head pin, string a spacer, a coin bead, and a spacer. Make a wrapped loop (Basics, p. 6).

On a head pin, string a bicone crystal. Make a wrapped loop. Make eight bicone units.

2 Cut a 3½-in. (8.9 cm) piece of chain. Open a jump ring (Basics). Attach four bicone units, the coin-bead unit, four bicone units, and the chain. Close the jump ring.

3 Open the loop of an earring wire (Basics) and attach the dangle. Close the loop. Make a second earring to match the first.

Supply List

- **2** 12 mm faceted coin beads
- **16** 4 mm bicone crystals, **2** each in **4** colors
- **4** 1 mm round spacers
- **7** in. (18 cm) long-and-short-link chain, 4–8 mm links
- **18** 2-in. (5 cm) head pins
- **2** 8 mm decorative jump rings
- pair of earring wires
- chainnose pliers
- roundnose pliers
- diagonal wire cutters

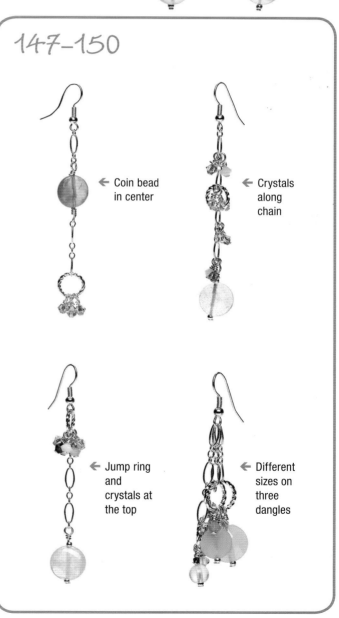

147–150

← Coin bead in center

← Crystals along chain

← Jump ring and crystals at the top

← Different sizes on three dangles

Lucite blooms

Lucite flower beads are so lightweight that a big bouquet won't strain your ears, but so nicely detailed that a single blossom will do just as well. Let a blooming spring landscape inspire your own variations on the floral theme. — *Cathy Jakicic*

151

1 On a decorative head pin, string a bicone crystal, a 14 mm flower bead, and a 16 mm flower bead. Bend the head pin at a right angle.

2 Make a plain loop (Basics, p. 6) behind the flower beads.

3 Cut a 1-in. (2.5 cm) piece of chain. Open the loop and attach the chain. Close the loop.

4 Open the loop of an earring wire (Basics) and attach the dangle. Close the loop. Make a second earring to match the first.

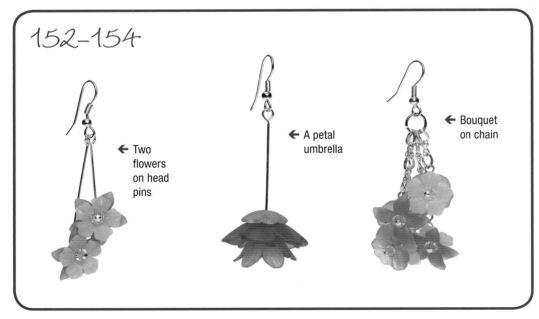

152–154

← Two flowers on head pins

← A petal umbrella

← Bouquet on chain

Supply List

Lucite flowers from The Bead Farm, beadfarm.com.

- **2** 16 mm Lucite flower beads
- **2** 14 mm Lucite flower beads
- **2** 4 mm bicone crystals
- **3** in. (7.6 cm) figaro chain, 1–3 mm links
- **2** 2-in. (5 cm) decorative head pins
- pair of earring wires
- chainnose pliers
- roundnose pliers
- diagonal wire cutters

Mother's Day

Mother's Day opens up a wealth of possibilities for jewelry gifts for mom. Use crystals to commemorate the birthdays of children, or give her tiny photos of her pride and joy. Hobby-specific charms accented with her birthstone are also a personal touch. And mother-of-pearl is always appropriate. Those pearls didn't raise themselves, after all. — *Cathy Jakicic*

155

1 On a decorative head pin, string ten crystals of the same color. Make the first half of a wrapped loop (Basics, p. 6). Repeat for the desired number of dangles.

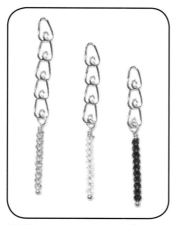

2 Cut a piece of chain for each dangle, varying the length of each slightly. The longest piece should be 1 in. (2.5 cm). Attach a bead unit to each chain and complete the wraps.

3 Open the loop of an earring wire (Basics) and attach the dangles. Close the loop. Make a second earring in the mirror image of the first.

Supply List

Chain and charms from Fusion Beads, fusionbeads.com.

- **20** 2 mm round crystals for each child represented
- 2 in. (5 cm) pretzel chain, 7 mm links, for each child represented
- **2** 2-in. (5 cm) decorative head pins for each child represented
- pair of earring wires
- chainnose pliers
- roundnose pliers
- diagonal wire cutters

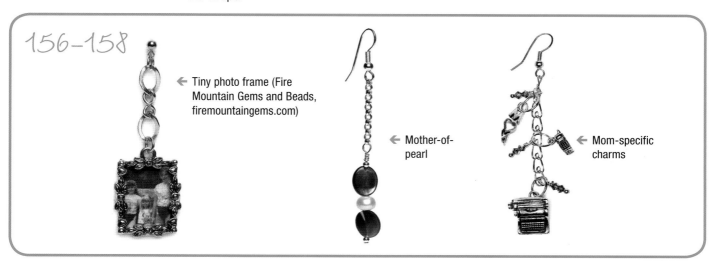

156–158

← Tiny photo frame (Fire Mountain Gems and Beads, firemountaingems.com)

← Mother-of-pearl

← Mom-specific charms

45

Shells

Shell beads and components make short work of summery earrings. Not only are shells lightweight and comfortable to wear, but they're affordable, too. — *Lindsay Mikulsky*

159

1 On a head pin, string a curly shell bead and make the first half of a wrapped loop (Basics, p. 6).

Cut a ¼-in. (6 mm) piece of chain. Attach the shell unit to the chain and complete the wraps.

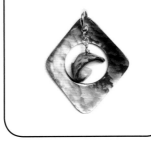

2 Open a 6 mm jump ring (Basics). Attach the chain and a diamond-shaped shell bead. Close the jump ring.

3 Use a 4 mm jump ring to attach the 6 mm jump ring to the loop of an earring wire. Make a second earring to match the first.

Supply List

Shells from Beads & Pieces, beadsandpieces.com.

- **2** diamond-shaped shell beads, approximately 30 mm
- **2** 8–10 mm curly shell beads
- ½ in. (1.3 cm) chain, 3 mm links
- **2** 1½-in. (3.8 cm) head pins
- **2** 6 mm jump rings
- **2** 4 mm jump rings
- pair of earring wires
- chainnose pliers
- roundnose pliers
- diagonal wire cutters

160–162

← Curly shells on hoops

← Silver-framed shells

← 30 mm shell disks

Ring engagement

Decorative rings are so beautiful and versatile, they're easy to fall in love with. Combine them with different materials to make your own one-of-a-kind union. Your earrings can be elegant or whimsical, simple or ornate. — *Cathy Jakicic*

163

1 Cut two 2-in. (5 cm) pieces of smaller-link chain and one 1-in. (2.5 cm) piece of larger-link chain.

2 Open a jump ring (Basics, p. 6) and attach a hammered ring to a 1-in. (2.5 cm) chain. Repeat with a 2-in. (5 cm) chain.

3 Open the loop of an earring wire (Basics). Attach the chains. Close the loop. Make a second earring to match the first.

Supply List

All rings from Oriental Trading Company, orientaltrading.com.

- **4** 23 mm hammered rings
- **8** in. (20 cm) chain, 2–3 mm links
- **2** in. (5 cm) chain, 4–5 mm links
- **4** 7 mm jump rings
- pair of earring wires
- chainnose pliers
- roundnose pliers
- diagonal wire cutters

164-169

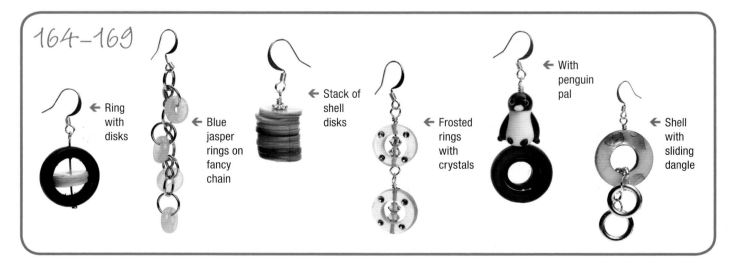

← Ring with disks

← Blue jasper rings on fancy chain

← Stack of shell disks

← Frosted rings with crystals

← With penguin pal

← Shell with sliding dangle

Bead caps

Bead caps and cones with looped edges set the stage for intricate earrings. Both findings come in a variety of styles with different numbers of loops, so before you buy your crystals, be sure to calculate how many you'll actually need. — *Anna Elizabeth Draeger*

170

1 On a head pin, string a 3 mm bicone crystal and make a plain loop (Basics, p. 6). Make eight to 18 3 mm-bicone units.

On a head pin, string a 4 mm bicone crystal and make a plain loop. Make four to nine 4 mm-bicone units.

2 Open the loop of a 3 mm-bicone unit (Basics) and attach it to a loop on a bead cap. Close the loop. Repeat until you've attached a 3 mm-bicone unit to each of the bead cap's loops.

Open the loop of a 4 mm-bicone unit and attach it to a loop on a cone. Repeat until you've attached a 4 mm-bicone unit to each of the cone's loops.

3 Cut a 1-in. (2.5 cm) piece of chain. On one end, attach a 4 mm-bicone unit. On the next link, attach two 3 mm-bicone units. Attach two 3 mm-bicone units to the next link.

4 Cut a 2-in. (5 cm) piece of wire. Make a plain loop on one end. Open the loop and attach the chain. Close the loop. On the wire, string: cone, 3 mm bicone, 4 mm bicone, 3 mm, bead cap, 3 mm. Make a plain loop.

Supply List

- **10–20** 4 mm bicone crystals
- **22–42** 3 mm bicone crystals
- **2** 8–10 mm bead caps, with loops
- **2** 10–12 mm cones, with loops
- **4 in. (10 cm)** 24-gauge half-hard wire
- 2 in. (5 cm) chain, 2 mm links
- **24–54** 1½-in. (3.8 cm) 24-gauge head pins
- pair of earring wires
- chainnose pliers
- roundnose pliers
- diagonal wire cutters

5 Open the loop of an earring wire (Basics). Attach the dangle and close the loop. Make a second earring to match the first.

171–175

← Dangles attached to a bead cap

← Briolette nestled inside a cone

← Chain draped from a cone

← Bead cap over an 8 mm crystal

← Three bead caps

Charms

Charm bracelets are a perennial favorite. Why not make a pair of earrings to match? You can express your school spirit, represent a cherished hobby, or take part in pirate mania. Or, show off your astrological sign with a zodiac charm paired with your birthstone. — *Lindsay Mikulsky*

176

Supply List

- letter charms, approximately 8 mm
- **2** 8 mm round crystals
- **22–26** 4 mm round crystals, in two colors
- 3 in. (7.6 cm) chain, 3–4 mm links
- **22–26** 1-in. (2.5 cm) head pins
- 4 mm jump rings, one for each letter charm
- pair of earring-wire blanks
- chainnose pliers
- roundnose pliers
- diagonal wire cutters

1 On a head pin, string an 8 mm crystal. Make a plain loop (Basics, p. 6). Repeat with all but two of the remaining crystals. Set these two crystals aside for step 4.

2 Cut a 1½-in. (3.8 cm) piece of chain. On your work space, arrange your letter charms next to the chain. Open a jump ring (Basics) and attach a charm and a link. Close the jump ring. Repeat with the remaining charms.

3 Attach 4 mm-crystal units to the chain, one per link, including the links with a letter charm. On the bottom link, attach an 8 mm-crystal unit.

4 String a 4 mm crystal on an earring-wire blank. Make a plain loop next to the crystal. Open the loop (Basics) and attach the dangle. Close the loop. Repeat steps 2–4 to make a second earring.

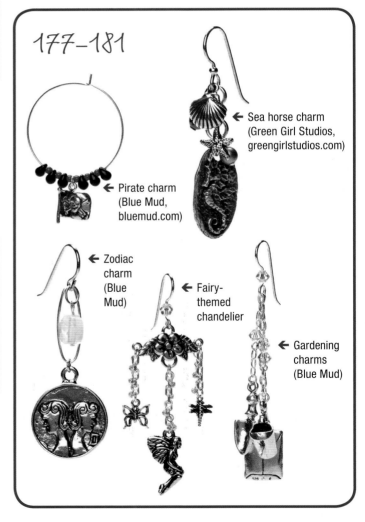

177–181

← Sea horse charm (Green Girl Studios, greengirlstudios.com)

← Pirate charm (Blue Mud, bluemud.com)

← Zodiac charm (Blue Mud)

← Fairy-themed chandelier

← Gardening charms (Blue Mud)

Kite-shaped chandeliers

Kite-shaped chandelier findings make simple frames for a variety of crystals. You can showcase large teardrops or dangle dainty bicones from fine chain. Whether you opt for a bold or breezy look, these findings will be the perfect backdrop. — *Karla Schafer*

182

1 On a crystal head pin, string a crystal teardrop. Make a plain loop (Basics, p. 6).

2 Open the head pin's loop (Basics) and attach it to the inside loop of a kite-shaped chandelier finding. Close the loop.

3 Open the loop of an earring wire (Basics). Attach the dangle and close the loop. Make a second earring to match the first.

Supply List

All supplies from Auntie's Beads, auntiesbeads.com.

- **2** 24 mm crystal teardrops
- **2** 42 mm kite-shaped chandelier findings
- **2** 1½-in. (3.8 cm) crystal head pins
- pair of earring wires
- chainnose pliers
- roundnose pliers
- diagonal wire cutters

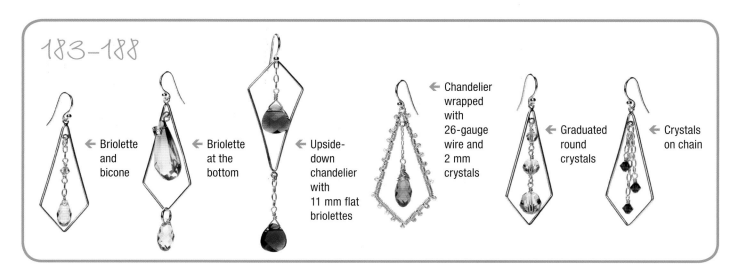

183–188

← Briolette and bicone

← Briolette at the bottom

← Upside-down chandelier with 11 mm flat briolettes

← Chandelier wrapped with 26-gauge wire and 2 mm crystals

← Graduated round crystals

← Crystals on chain

Cubic zirconia coins

Cubic zirconia (CZ) coins in cheery colors brighten up these earrings. They have a single top-drilled hole that accommodates jump rings, making it easy to incorporate them into a variety of designs. — *Lindsay Mikulsky*

189

1 On a head pin, string a crystal drop. Make the first half of a wrapped loop (Basics, p. 6).

Cut a 1¾-in. (4.4 cm) piece of chain. Attach the drop to the center link and complete the wraps.

2 Open a 6 mm jump ring (Basics). Attach one end of the chain, a cubic zirconia coin, and the other end of the chain. Close the jump ring.

3 Use a 4 mm jump ring to attach the dangle and the loop of an earring wire. Make a second earring to match the first.

Supply List

- **2** 16 mm cubic zirconia coins
- **2** 9 mm crystal drops
- 3½ in. (8.9 cm) chain, 2–4 mm links
- **2** 2-in. (5 cm) head pins
- **2** 6 mm jump rings
- **2** 4 mm jump rings
- pair of earring wires
- chainnose pliers
- roundnose pliers
- diagonal wire cutters

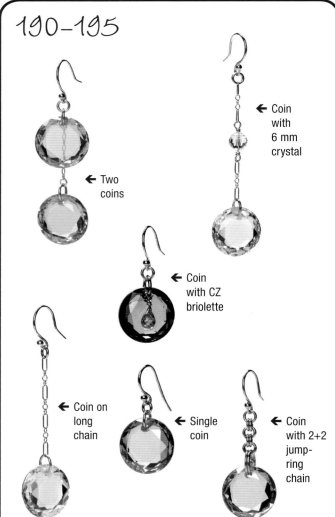

190–195

← Coin with 6 mm crystal

← Two coins

← Coin with CZ briolette

← Coin on long chain

← Single coin

← Coin with 2+2 jump-ring chain

Lightweight Lucite

Lucite's light weight makes it ideal for big earrings. Try classic round beads in bold colors, or opt for fruit or drops adorned with chain. — *Naomi Fujimoto*

196

1 On a head pin, string a 14 mm bead. Make a plain loop (Basics, p. 6).

2 Cut a 1¼-in. (3.2 cm) piece of wire. Make a plain loop on one end. String an 8 mm bead and make a plain loop. Repeat to make a 10 mm-bead unit.

3 Open the loops of the 10 mm-bead unit (Basics). Attach the 8 mm-bead unit to one loop and the 14 mm-bead unit to the other. Close the loops.

4 Open the loop of an earring post (Basics). Attach the dangle and close the loop. Make a second earring to match the first.

Supply note
Because the holes in Lucite beads are often large, use head pins with large heads.

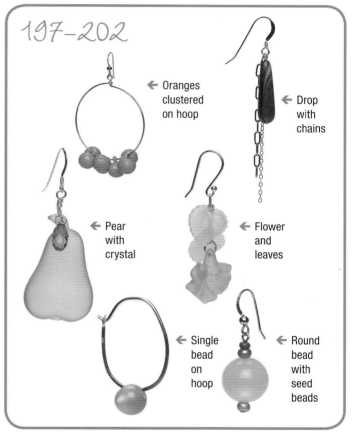

197–202

← Oranges clustered on hoop

← Drop with chains

← Pear with crystal

← Flower and leaves

← Single bead on hoop

← Round bead with seed beads

Supply List

All Lucite beads from The Beadin' Path, beadinpath.com.

- **2** 14 mm round Lucite beads
- **2** 10 mm round Lucite beads
- **2** 8 mm round Lucite beads
- **5** in. (13 cm) 22-gauge half-hard wire
- **2** 1½-in. (3.8 cm) head pins
- pair of earring posts with ear nuts
- chainnose pliers
- roundnose pliers
- diagonal wire cutters

Star power

Show your megawatt style with easy star-shaped earrings. Metal tube beads are always a good option — try Hill Tribes silver for its earthy, oxidized finish. Vintage tubes in a funky color are also fun. If you use glass beads, bend the wire carefully to avoid breaking the beads. — *Monica Han*

203

1 Cut a 9-in. (23 cm) piece of wire. String a tube bead, leaving 2 in. (5 cm) of wire above the bead. Bend the wire next to the bead. String nine more tubes, bending the wire next to each bead to form a star shape.

2 Bend the wire's longer end upward to make a stem. Wrap the shorter end around the stem as in a wrapped loop (Basics, p. 6).

3 Make a wrapped loop.

4 Open the loop of an earring wire (Basics). Attach the dangle and close the loop. Make a second earring to match the first.

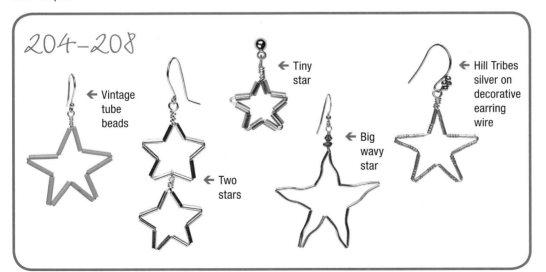

204-208

← Vintage tube beads

← Tiny star

← Two stars

← Big wavy star

← Hill Tribes silver on decorative earring wire

Supply List

- **20** 10–12 mm tube beads (Fire Mountain Gems and Beads, firemountaingems.com)
- 18 in. (46 cm) 22-gauge half-hard wire
- pair of earring wires
- chainnose pliers
- roundnose pliers
- diagonal wire cutters

Metal spirals

Sterling silver and gold-filled curls will keep you spiraling in control. They're available in different lengths, so you can go super long with huge crystals or wear shorter spirals with briolettes for a less flashy look. — *Naomi Fujimoto*

209

1 On a head pin, string a crystal. Make a plain loop (Basics, p. 6).

2 Open the loop (Basics) and attach a spiral connector. Close the loop.

3 Open the loop (Basics) of an earring wire. Attach the dangle and close the loop. Make a second earring in the mirror image of the first.

Supply List

All spiral connectors from Rings & Things, rings-things.com.

- **2** 18 mm crystals
- **2** 64 mm spiral connectors
- **2** 1½-in. (3.8 cm) head pins
- pair of earring wires
- chainnose pliers
- roundnose pliers
- diagonal wire cutters

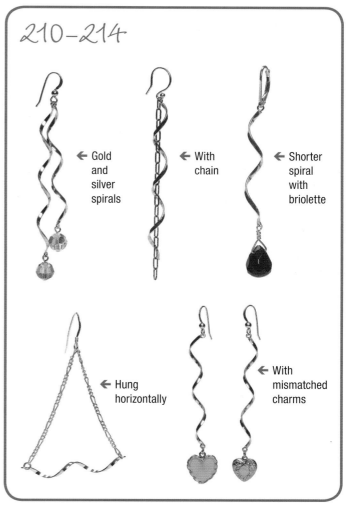

210–214

← Gold and silver spirals

← With chain

← Shorter spiral with briolette

← Hung horizontally

← With mismatched charms

55

Crystals and chain

These earrings have a little of everything — a whimsical wire link, a remnant of chain, and sparkling crystal dangles. For variation, change the gauge of the wire, the length of the chain, or the shape of the crystals.

— *Anna Elizabeth Draeger*

215

1 Cut a 2-in. (5 cm) piece of wire. Curve the wire around a pen barrel.

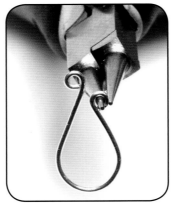

2 Using roundnose pliers, make a small loop on one end. Make a loop on the other end, asymmetrical to the first loop.

3 On a head pin, string a 3 mm bicone crystal, a butterfly crystal, and a 3 mm bicone. Make a plain loop (Basics, p. 6).

4 On a head pin, string a 3 mm bicone and make a plain loop. Repeat to make a total of two 3 mm-bicone units and two 4 mm-bicone units.

Supply List

- **2** 6 mm butterfly crystals (Artbeads.com)
- **4** 4 mm bicone crystals
- **8** 3 mm bicone crystals
- **4** in. (10 cm) 20-gauge half-hard wire
- **10** 1-in. (2.5 cm) head pins
- 1–2 in. (2.5–5 cm) long-and-short–link chain, 3–4 mm links
- pair of earring wires
- chainnose pliers
- roundnose pliers
- diagonal wire cutters

5 Cut a ½–1-in. (1.3–2.5 cm) piece of chain. String the chain on the link. Open the loop of the butterfly unit and attach the bottom link. Close the loop. Attach each 3 mm-bicone unit and each 4 mm-bicone unit to links as desired.

6 Open the loop of an earring wire (Basics). Attach the dangle and close the loop. Make a second earring in the mirror image of the first.

216–219

← 18-gauge link and larger butterfly

← Hammered link at bottom of chain

← Large link with briolette and bicones

← Hammered link and one large crystal

Big stones

Chunky nuggets aren't just for necklaces and bracelets. When used sparingly, they make striking focal points in earrings. Simple designs work best — accented with a bit of chain or a single jump ring, these rocks won't weigh you down. — *Naomi Fujimoto*

220

1 On a bench block or anvil, hammer a soldered jump ring. Flip the jump ring over and hammer the other side.

2 Cut a 4-in. (10 cm) piece of wire. With the largest part of your roundnose pliers, make the first half of a wrapped loop (Basics, p. 6). Attach the jump ring and complete the wraps.

3 String a nugget bead and make a wrapped loop perpendicular to the first loop.

4 Open the loop of an earring wire (Basics). Attach the dangle and close the loop. Make a second earring to match the first.

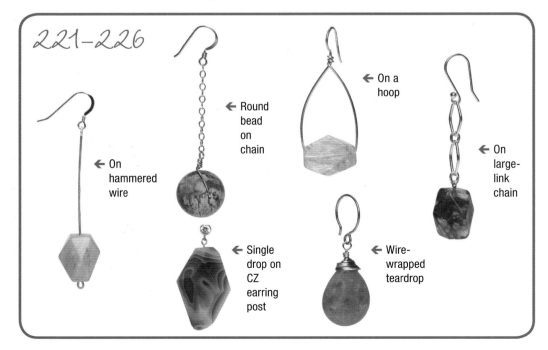

221-226

← On hammered wire

← Round bead on chain

← Single drop on CZ earring post

← On a hoop

← Wire-wrapped teardrop

← On large-link chain

Supply List

- **2** 17–20 mm faceted nugget beads
- 8 in. (20 cm) 22-gauge half-hard wire
- **2** 18 mm soldered jump rings
- pair of earring wires
- chainnose pliers
- roundnose pliers
- diagonal wire cutters
- bench block or anvil
- hammer

Fruitful fun

Summer's harvest is plentiful, so getting your recommended daily dose of fruit is easy. You'll have so much fun making fruit earrings, you won't want to stop after just one serving. — *Stacie Thompson*

227

1 On a head pin, string a round bead and a dagger bead. Using the largest part of your roundnose pliers, roll a loop at the end of the wire. Leave space between the dagger and the loop.

2 String the dangle on an earring wire. With chainnose pliers, gently squeeze the earring wire's loop. Make a second earring to match the first.

228–233

← Long silver earring wire with blueberry bead (Elizabeth Johnson, sonoranbeads.com)

← Arched brass earring wire with peach bead (Elizabeth Johnson)

← Bead-capped strawberry

← Gold leaves with pear (J.P. Imported, jpimported.com)

← Crystal with glass lemon

← Leaf charm and grapes

Butterflies and leaves

Net a variety of colorful butterfly beads. You can make yours even more distinctive by including earring threads, chain, or fancy links. — *Jane Konkel*

234

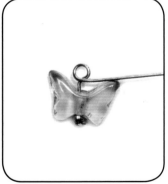

1 On a head pin, string a spacer and a butterfly bead. Make the first half of a wrapped loop (Basics, p. 6).

2 Cut a ½-in. (1.3 cm) piece of chain. Attach the bead unit and complete the wraps. If desired, make a coil (Basics) with the excess wire.

3 Cut a 2½-in. (6.4 cm) piece of wire. On one end, make a coil. String a leaf bead and make a plain loop perpendicular to the coil. Make a second leaf unit in another color.

4 Open the loop of a leaf unit (Basics) and attach the chain and a jump ring. Close the loop.

5 Open the loop of the remaining leaf unit. Attach the jump ring. Close the loop.

6 Open the loop of an earring wire (Basics) and attach the dangle. Close the loop. Make a second earring to match the first.

Supply List

- **2** 12 mm butterfly beads
- **4** 11 mm leaf beads, in two colors
- **2** 3 mm spacers
- **10** in. (25 cm) 24-gauge half-hard wire
- **1** in. (2.5 cm) chain, 2–3 mm links
- **2** 2-in. (5 cm) head pins
- **2** 4–5 mm decorative jump rings
- pair of earring wires
- chainnose pliers
- roundnose pliers
- diagonal wire cutters

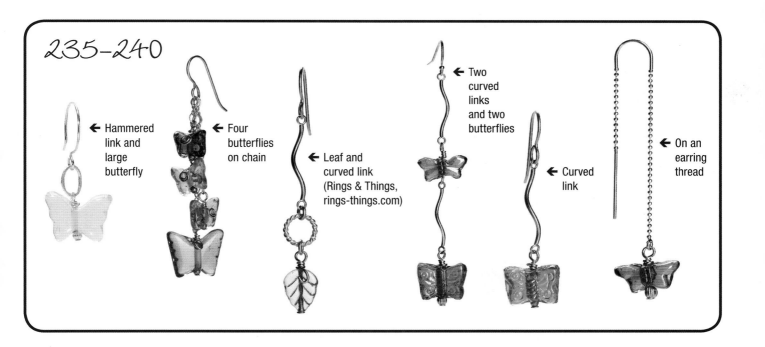

235-240

← Hammered link and large butterfly

← Four butterflies on chain

← Leaf and curved link (Rings & Things, rings-things.com)

← Two curved links and two butterflies

← Curved link

← On an earring thread

Natural chandeliers

Chandelier earring findings are no longer relegated to metals. Mother-of-pearl, shell, and wood are natural stand-ins for traditional gold, silver, copper, or brass. — *Irina Miech*

241

1 On a head pin, string a pearl and a 13º seed bead. Make the first half of a wrapped loop (Basics, p. 6). Attach a hole of a chandelier finding and complete the wraps.

2 Cut a 2½-in. (6.4 cm) piece of wire. Make the first half of a wrapped loop. Attach the remaining hole of the chandelier finding and complete the wraps.

3 String a small pearl and a 13º. Make a wrapped loop perpendicular to the first loop.

4 Open the loop of an earring wire (Basics) and attach the dangle. Close the loop. Make a second earring to match the first.

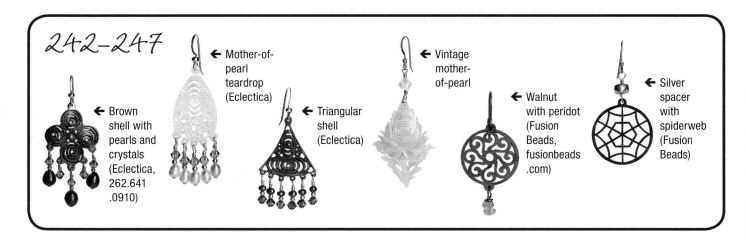

242–247

← Brown shell with pearls and crystals (Eclectica, 262.641.0910)

← Mother-of-pearl teardrop (Eclectica)

← Triangular shell (Eclectica)

← Vintage mother-of-pearl

← Walnut with peridot (Fusion Beads, fusionbeads.com)

← Silver spacer with spiderweb (Fusion Beads)

Wire-wrapped flowers

Wire wrap six petals and a single round center bead to form pretty flower earrings. Try teardrops or twisted or faceted ovals. — *Monica Han*

248

1 Cut a 16-in. (41 cm) piece of wire. Center a petal-shaped pearl, a round pearl, and a petal on the wire.

2 On each end, pull the wire around the back of the petal. Make one or two wraps between the round pearl and the petal.

3 On each end, string a petal. Pull the wire around the back of the petal. Make one or two wraps between the round pearl and the petal.

4 On one end, repeat step 3. On the remaining end, string a petal and make a wrapped loop (Basics, p. 6). Pull the wire around the back of the bead. Make one or two wraps between the round pearl and the petal.

5 Weave each end between each petal and around each wrap. Trim the excess wire and tuck the ends.

6 Open the loop of an earring wire (Basics) and attach the dangle. Close the loop. Make a second earring to match the first.

Supply List

- **12** 11–13 mm petal-shaped pearls
- **2** 6 mm round pearls
- **32 in.** (81 cm) 26-gauge soft wire
- pair of earring wires
- chainnose pliers
- roundnose pliers
- diagonal wire cutters

249-251

← Twisted ovals, crystal, and gold wire

← Faceted ovals and decorative earring wire

← Twisted ovals, pearl, and silver wire

Briolettes and coiled wire

Faceted briolettes make beautiful drop earrings. Instead of connecting them with simple wire wraps, try making coils and scrolls as a decorative alternative. — *Anna Elizabeth Draeger*

252

1 On a decorative head pin, string a briolette. Bend the wire above the top of the bead. Make a coil (Basics, p. 6), centering it above the bead.

2 Cut a 2½-in. (6.4 cm) piece of wire. Make a coil on one end. String a bicone crystal and make a coil on the remaining end, in the opposite direction.

3 Open a jump ring (Basics), and attach the briolette unit and the scroll unit. Close the jump ring.

4 Open the loop of an earring wire (Basics) and attach the dangle. Close the loop. Make a second earring.

253-257

← On a crystal-studded head pin

← Coil and cubic zirconia

← Scroll and labradorite briolette

← Coil and amazonite

← Hammered coil and chrysoprase

Supply List

- 2 14 mm gemstone briolettes
- 2 4 mm bicone crystals
- 5 in. (13 cm) 24-gauge half-hard wire
- 2 2-in. (5 cm) decorative head pins
- 2 5 mm jump rings
- pair of earring wires
- chainnose pliers
- roundnose pliers
- diagonal wire cutters

Stacking earring wires

Use specially shaped "stacking" earring wires to make quick work of simple earrings. Just trim the ball from an earring wire, string your beads, and make a plain loop. An easy dangle finishes it off in style. If you prefer to skip the dangle, hammer the end of the wire to keep your beads in place. — *Lindsay Mikulsky*

258

1 Trim the 2 mm ball from the end of a stacking earring wire. On the earring wire, string: bicone crystal, pearl, bicone, pearl, bicone. Make a plain loop (Basics, p. 6).

2 On a head pin, string a bicone and a pearl. Make a plain loop. Open the loop (Basics) and attach the bead unit to the earring wire. Close the loop. Make a second earring to match the first.

Supply List

- **6** 4 mm pearls
- **8** 3 mm bicone crystals
- **2** 1-in. (2.5 cm) head pins
- pair of stacking earring wires (Artbeads.com)
- chainnose pliers
- roundnose pliers
- diagonal wire cutters

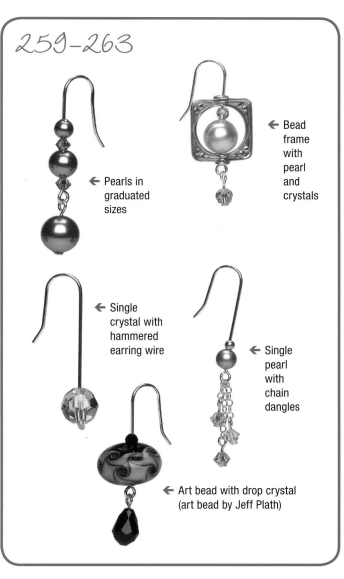

259-263

← Pearls in graduated sizes

← Bead frame with pearl and crystals

← Single crystal with hammered earring wire

← Single pearl with chain dangles

← Art bead with drop crystal (art bead by Jeff Plath)

Versatile squares

Double-drilled square beads lend themselves to multiple design options and shine when paired with chain and crystals. — *Sara Strauss*

264

1 Cut a 3-in. (7.6 cm) piece of wire. Make a wrapped loop (Basics, p. 6) in the center of the wire. Do not trim the excess wire.

2 String a double-drilled square bead on both ends of the wire. On each end, make a plain loop (Basics) perpendicular to the first loop.

3 Cut a 1-in. (2.5 cm) piece of wire. Make a plain loop on one end. String a 4 mm bead and make a plain loop. Repeat.

On a head pin, string an 8 mm bead. Make a plain loop. Repeat.

4 Cut a 1-in. (2.5 cm) and a ¾-in. (1.9 cm) piece of chain. Open the loops (Basics) of the square-bead unit. Attach a chain to each loop and close the loops.

Open the loops of each 4 mm-bead unit. On one end, attach a chain. On the other end, attach an 8 mm-bead unit. Close the loops.

Supply List

- **2** 10–14 mm square beads, double drilled (Rings & Things, rings-things.com)
- **4** 8 mm round beads
- **4** 4 mm round beads
- 10 in. (25 cm) 24-gauge half-hard wire
- 3½ in. (8.9 cm) chain, 2–4 mm links
- **4** 1½-in. (3.8 cm) head pins
- pair of earring wires
- chainnose pliers
- roundnose pliers
- diagonal wire cutters

5 Open the loop of an earring wire (Basics). Attach the dangle and close the loop. Make a second earring in the mirror image of the first.

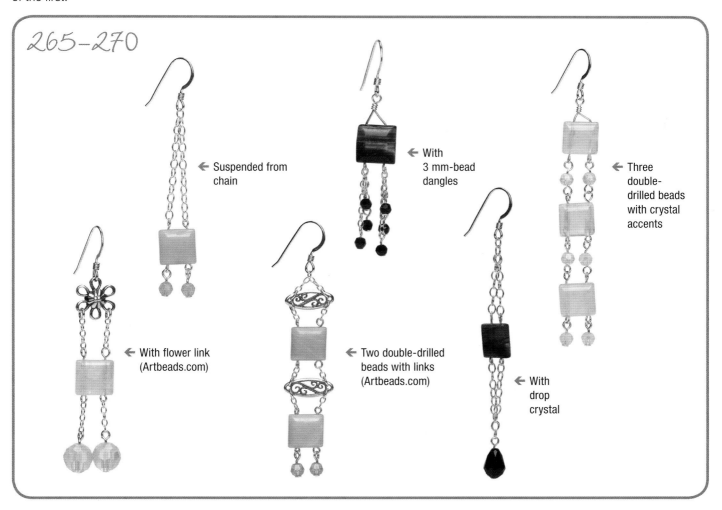

265-270

← Suspended from chain

← With 3 mm-bead dangles

← Three double-drilled beads with crystal accents

← With flower link (Artbeads.com)

← Two double-drilled beads with links (Artbeads.com)

← With drop crystal

Fringe beads

Tiny top-drilled fringe beads are available in many colors. Whether you string them on wire, head pins, or flexible beading wire, they add a playful tone to any pair of earrings. — *Lindsay Mikulsky*

271

1 Cut a 1-in. (2.5 cm) piece of chain. Open a jump ring (Basics, p. 6) and attach a fringe bead and one end of the chain. Close the jump ring.

2 Using jump rings, attach a fringe bead to each link of chain. To create a spiral pattern, alternate the side of the links you attach the beads to.

3 Open the loop of an earring wire (Basics). Attach the dangle and close the loop. Make a second earring to match the first.

Supply List

- **16–24** 4 mm fringe beads
- 2 in. (5 cm) chain, 3–4 mm links
- **16–24** 3–4 mm jump rings
- pair of earring wires
- chainnose and roundnose pliers, or **2** pairs of chainnose pliers
- diagonal wire cutters

272–276

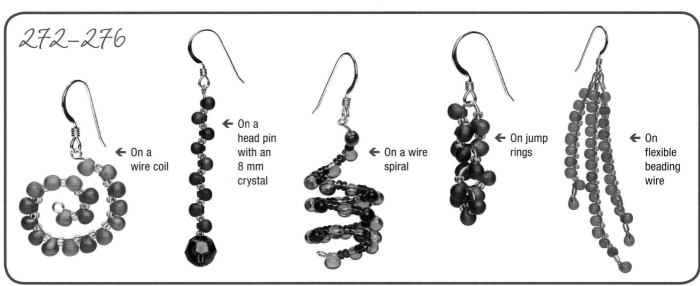

← On a wire coil

← On a head pin with an 8 mm crystal

← On a wire spiral

← On jump rings

← On flexible beading wire

Decorative chain

Decorative chain with double-ring links makes earrings look more complicated than they are. It'll be your little secret that you made these in less than 10 minutes.

— *Sue Godfrey*

277

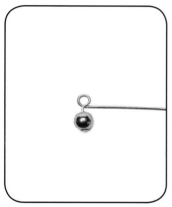

1 On a head pin, string a round bead. Make the first half of a wrapped loop (Basics, p. 6).

2 Cut a 1-in. (2.5 cm) piece of chain that has two pairs of double-ring links. Attach the bead unit to one end and complete the wraps.

3 Open the loop of an earring wire (Basics). Attach the chain and close the loop. Make a second earring to match the first.

Supply List

All supplies from Midwest Beads, midwestbeads.com.

- **2** 4–5 mm round beads
- 2 in. (5 cm) decorative chain, 5–7 mm links
- **2** 1½-in. (3.8 cm) head pins
- pair of earring wires
- chainnose pliers
- roundnose pliers
- diagonal wire cutters

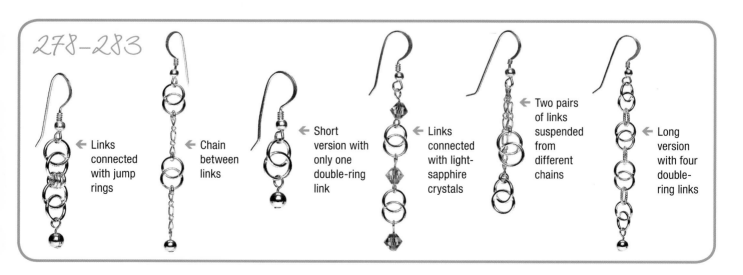

278-283

← Links connected with jump rings

← Chain between links

← Short version with only one double-ring link

← Links connected with light-sapphire crystals

← Two pairs of links suspended from different chains

← Long version with four double-ring links

Large jump rings

Large decorative jump rings are a simple addition to basic earrings. They make great frames for your beads, or you can use them as links for chain and bead units. — *Lindsay Mikulsky*

284

1 On a head pin, string a round bead and make a plain loop (Basics, p. 6).

2 Open a 4–5 mm jump ring (Basics). Attach the bead unit, a 12–16 mm jump ring, and a closed 4–5 mm jump ring. Close the jump ring.

3 Open the loop of an earring wire (Basics). Attach the dangle and close the loop. Make a second earring to match the first.

Supply List

- **2** 6–8 mm round beads
- **2** 1-in. (2.5 cm) head pins
- **2** 12–16 mm decorative jump rings
- **4** 4–5 mm jump rings
- pair of earring wires
- chainnose pliers
- roundnose pliers
- diagonal wire cutters

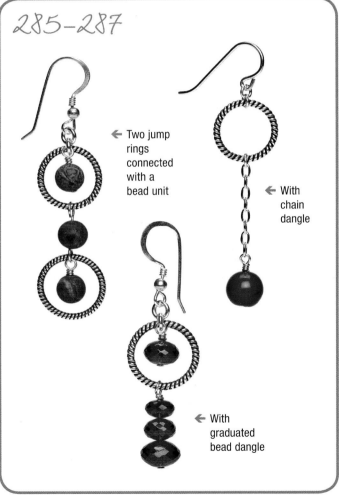

285-287

← Two jump rings connected with a bead unit

← With chain dangle

← With graduated bead dangle

Faceted and fine

Strung with faceted beads, such as these briolettes, delicate earrings are always in style. Refer to "Making your own earring wires," p. 12, if you'd like to try some DIY wirework. — *Jane Konkel*

288

1 Cut a 10-in. (25 cm) piece of wire. String a briolette and make a set of wraps above it (Basics, p. 6). Make the first half of a wrapped loop (Basics) above the wraps.

2 Grasp the loop with chainnose pliers. Using your fingers, wrap the wire over the top of the briolette and back toward the loop, overlapping the wraps.

3 Open the loop of an earring wire (Basics). Attach the dangle and close the loop.

4 If desired, string a spacer on the earring wire. Make a second earring to match the first.

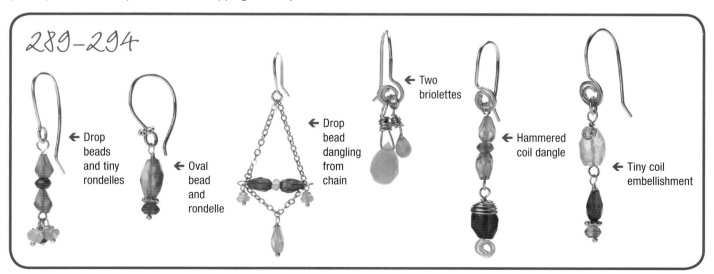

289-294

← Drop beads and tiny rondelles

← Oval bead and rondelle

← Drop bead dangling from chain

← Two briolettes

← Hammered coil dangle

← Tiny coil embellishment

Autumn copper

For fall, my metal of choice is copper. It's relatively soft and therefore easy to shape. To make symmetrical components, work with wires in pairs. Copper's earthy color makes it ideal for hammering, and it takes on a graceful patina. If you have sensitive ears, accent copper dangles with gold or silver earring wires and coordinating bead caps or spacers. — *Jane Konkel*

295

1 Cut a 5-in. (13 cm) piece of 20-gauge wire. Center the wire on a mandrel. Pull the wire around the mandrel, forming an X. On each end, make a loop.

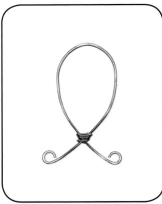

2 Cut a 3-in. (7.6 cm) piece of 22-gauge wire. Wrap it snugly around the X. Trim the excess wire and use chainnose pliers to tuck in the ends. On a bench block or anvil, hammer each side of the component.

3 On a head pin, string a color A bicone crystal, a bead cap, a color D rondelle, and a color B bicone. Make the first half of a wrapped loop (Basics, p. 6).

Make a second long bead unit, reversing the colors of the bicones and using a color E rondelle. Complete the wraps on this unit, wrapping over the top of the bicone.

4 On a head pin, string a color C bicone crystal, a bead cap, and a color E rondelle. Make the first half of a wrapped loop. Make two short bead units.

Make a third and a fourth short bead unit, using color B bicones and color D rondelles. Complete the wraps on these units, partially wrapping the tops of the rondelles.

5 Cut a 1½-in. (3.8 cm) piece of chain with an odd number of links. Attach a long bead unit to the center link. On each side of the long unit, skip one or two links and attach a short bead unit. Complete the wraps as you go.

6 Open each loop of the wire component. Attach an end link of the chain and a short bead unit to each loop. Close each loop.

7 Open the loop of an earring wire (Basics), and attach the dangle and a long bead unit. Close the loop. Make a second earring to match the first.

Supply List

- **12** 7 mm rondelles, **6** color D, **6** color E
- **16** 4 mm bicone crystals, **4** color A, **8** color B, **4** color C
- **12** 5 mm bead caps
- 10 in. (25 cm) 20-gauge half-hard wire
- 6 in. (15 cm) 22-gauge half-hard wire
- 3 in. (7.6 cm) chain, 2–3 mm links
- **12** 2-in. (5 cm) head pins
- pair of earring wires
- chainnose pliers
- roundnose pliers
- diagonal wire cutters
- bench block or anvil
- hammer
- mandrel or other cylindrical object

296-301

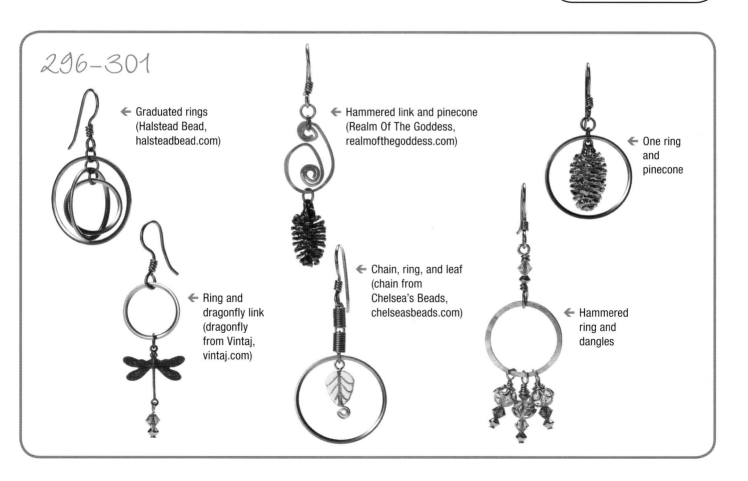

← Graduated rings (Halstead Bead, halsteadbead.com)

← Hammered link and pinecone (Realm Of The Goddess, realmofthegoddess.com)

← One ring and pinecone

← Ring and dragonfly link (dragonfly from Vintaj, vintaj.com)

← Chain, ring, and leaf (chain from Chelsea's Beads, chelseasbeads.com)

← Hammered ring and dangles

Colors that complement

You can design beautiful jewelry with just one color; adding another color, however, can really make things pop. To double the impact of your design, incorporate two complementary colors on opposite sides of the color wheel. — *Jane Konkel*

302

1 On a head pin, string a bicone crystal, a spacer, a rondelle, and a spacer. Make the first half of a wrapped loop (Basics, p. 6). Attach a soldered jump ring and complete the wraps.

2 Cut a 2½-in. (6.4 cm) piece of wire. Make the first half of a wrapped loop. Attach the jump ring and complete the wraps.

3 String a 10 mm bead. Make a wrapped loop.

4 Open the loop of an earring wire (Basics) and attach the dangle. Close the loop. Make a second earring to match the first.

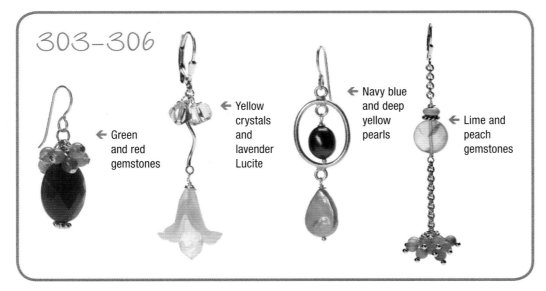

303-306

← Green and red gemstones

← Yellow crystals and lavender Lucite

← Navy blue and deep yellow pearls

← Lime and peach gemstones

Supply List

- **2** 10 mm blue glass beads
- **2** 8 mm brown rondelles
- **2** 4 mm blue bicone crystals
- **4** 4 mm spacers
- 5 in. (13 cm) 24-gauge half-hard wire
- **2** 2-in. (5 cm) head pins
- **2** 8 mm decorative soldered jump rings
- pair of earring wires
- chainnose pliers
- roundnose pliers
- diagonal wire cutters

Spook-tacular

Even if you're not crazy for Halloween, you're sure to see a few festive earrings in this collection that suit your scary side. No tricks here, just a week's worth of beaded treats. — *Jane Konkel*

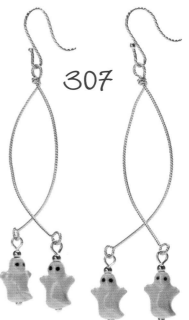

307

Supply List

- **4** 13 mm ceramic ghost beads (Rings & Things, rings-things.com)
- **4** 2 mm spacers
- 12 in. (30 cm) 20-gauge twisted wire
- **4** 1½-in. (3.8 cm) decorative head pins
- pair of twisted-wire earring wires
- chainnose pliers
- roundnose pliers
- diagonal wire cutters

1 On a decorative head pin, string a ghost bead and a spacer. Make a plain loop (Basics, p. 6). Make a second ghost-bead unit.

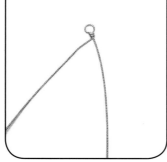

2 Cut a 6-in. (15 cm) piece of wire. About 2½ in. (6.4 cm) from one end, make a wrapped loop (Basics). Do not trim the excess wire.

3 On each end, make a plain loop. Open each loop (Basics) and attach a ghost-bead unit. Close the loop.

4 Bend each wire as desired. Open the loop of an earring wire (Basics) and attach the dangle. Close the loop. Make a second earring to match the first.

308-313

← Witch (cone, flat washer, round bead, rondelle, and teardrop)

← Bats and gunmetal chain (J.P. Imported, jpimported.com)

← Skull

← Magic wand

← Cat with evil-eye bow tie

← Crystal ball (round bead, disk, and flower)

DIY wire findings

These do-it-yourself findings are not only easy to make, they're economical, too. Use these earrings for ideas, or bend wires freestyle using your fingers and your imagination.

— *Jane Konkel*

314

1 On a decorative head pin, string a bead. Make the first half of a wrapped loop (Basics, p. 6). Make three bead units.

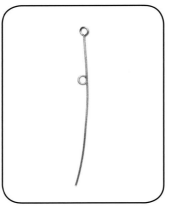

2 Cut a 3-in. (7.6 cm) piece of wire. Make a plain loop on one end (Basics). Place your roundnose pliers 1 in. (2.5 cm) from the loop, and pull the wire around the jaw to make a loop.

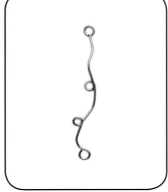

3 Make another loop ¾ in. (1.9 cm) from the previous loop. At the end of the wire, make a loop. Bend the wire into the desired shape.

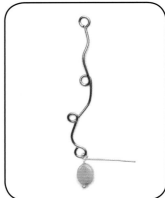

4 Attach a bead unit to each loop, completing the wraps as you go.

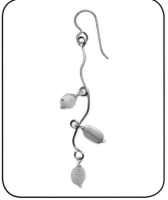

5 Open the loop of an earring wire (Basics). Attach the dangle and close the loop. Make a second earring in the mirror image of the first.

Supply List

- **6** 6–9 mm beads
- **6** in. (15 cm) 20-gauge half-hard wire
- **6** 1½-in. (3.8 cm) decorative head pins
- pair of earring wires
- chainnose pliers
- roundnose pliers
- diagonal wire cutters

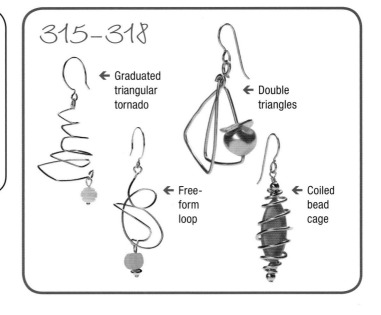

315–318

← Graduated triangular tornado

← Double triangles

← Free-form loop

← Coiled bead cage

Silver bonanza

Silver isn't just for accents and findings. When you give it a starring role, you can create earrings that shine for any occasion.

— *Cathy Jakicic*

319

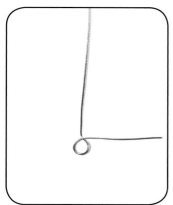

1 Cut a 4-in. (10 cm) piece of wire. Make the first half of a wrapped loop (Basics, p. 6) on one end.

2 Cut six 2-in. (5 cm) pieces of chain in assorted styles. Attach each to the loop and complete the wraps.

3 String a cone over the wire and chains. Make a wrapped loop.

4 Open the loop of an earring wire (Basics). Attach the dangle and close the loop. Make a second earring to match the first.

Supply List

- **2** 13 mm cones
- **12** 2-in. (5 cm) pieces of chain, assorted styles
- 8 in. (20 cm) 24-gauge half-hard wire
- pair of earring wires
- chainnose pliers
- roundnose pliers
- diagonal wire cutters

320–325

← Topaz crystal on head pin

← Graduated spacers

← Dangles on decorative jump rings

← Hearts on large jump ring

← Ornate focal bead

← Assorted spacers on large chain link

Lacy waves

WireLace gives hoops a flourish when you pair it with crystals. A few crystals and a blue motif give the earrings an aquatic look. Or, add more crystals and mix up the colors for a distinctly cha-cha feel. — *Linda Arline Hartung*

326

1 Cut a 6-in. (15 cm) piece of beading wire. Fold it in half to use as a needle. Cut an 18-in. (46 cm) piece of WireLace. Thread the lace through the needle, leaving a 6-in. (15 cm) tail. Over the needle, string a 12 mm crystal, leaving a ½-in. (1.3 cm) lace loop. Remove the needle.

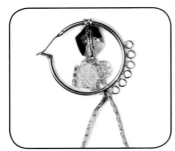

2 Slide the lace loop over a hoop earring and push the crystal against the hoop. Make an overhand knot (Basics, p. 6) next to the crystal, using the long lace strand. Pull apart a section of lace to make a wave. String both ends through the first loop on the hoop.

3 Pull apart a ¼-in. (6 mm) section of the long lace strand. String two bicone crystals. Pull apart another section of lace.

Supply List

- **2** 12 mm crystals
- **8** 6 mm bicone crystals, top drilled
- flexible beading wire, .010
- 1 yd. (.9 m) 6 mm WireLace
- pair of 1¼-in. (3.2 cm) hinged hoop earrings with seven loops
- diagonal wire cutters
- scissors
- G-S Hypo Cement

4a String the long strand through the second loop.
b Pull apart a section of lace and string the lace through the next loop.

5 Repeat step 4b until you've strung six loops. Repeat step 3 and tie an overhand knot through the last loop. Trim the excess lace.

6 Pull apart a section of the short lace strand.

7 Wrap the short lace strand around the hoop and tie an overhand knot near the crystal. Apply glue to each overhand knot. Make a second earring to match the first.

327

← More bicones, different colors

Easy wraps

Keep it simple and sparkling by wrapping fine wire and crystals around the elegant lines of a streamlined earring wire. Change the shape of the wire or the color of the crystal, but always make it simply sensational. Consider a single shimmering glass bead for a bolder look.

— *Amy Thompson*

328

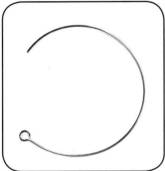

1 Cut a 4½-in. (11.4 cm) piece of 20-gauge wire. Make a plain loop (Basics, p. 6) on one end.

2 Cut an 8-in. (20 cm) piece of 26-gauge wire. Wrap it around the 20-gauge wire near the plain loop. Leave a short tail, and grasp it with pliers to keep the wraps taut. Make eight to 10 wraps.

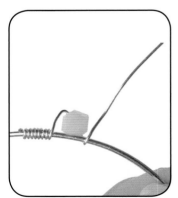

3 Make a bend in the 26-gauge wire ⅛ in. (3 mm) from the last wrap. String a bicone crystal. Wrap the 26-gauge wire around the 20-gauge wire eight to 10 times.

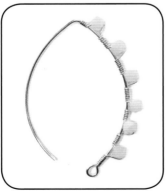

4 Repeat step 3 five times, ending with three or four wraps. Trim the excess 26-gauge wire and bend the 20-gauge wire as shown. Trim the excess wire, and file the end of the wire if necessary.

5 String a bicone on a head pin. Make a plain loop.

6 Open the loop of the bicone unit (Basics) and attach it to the loop of the earring wire. Close the loop. Make a second earring to match the first.

Supply List

- **14** 4 mm bicone crystals
- **9** in. (23 cm) 20-gauge half-hard wire
- **16** in. (41 cm) 26-gauge half-hard wire
- **2** 1½-in. (3.8 cm) head pins

- chainnose pliers
- roundnose pliers
- diagonal wire cutters
- metal file or emery board (optional)

329-334

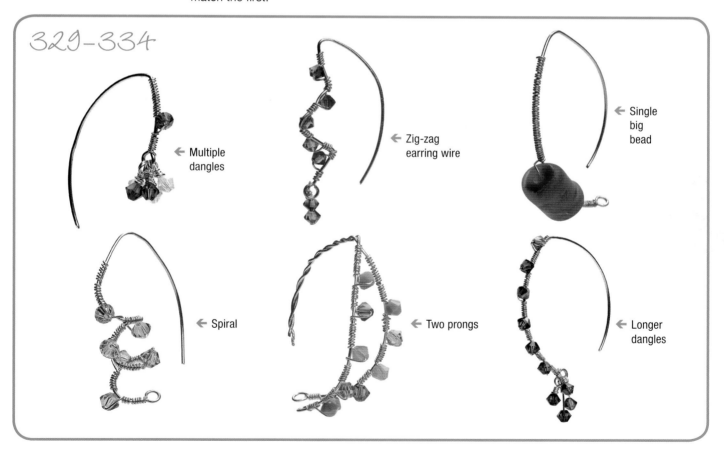

← Multiple dangles

← Zig-zag earring wire

← Single big bead

← Spiral

← Two prongs

← Longer dangles

Pretty porcelain

Porcelain beads range from primitive to proper and come in a number of colors, patterns, and sizes. Choose one that matches your personality, and you'll be a fashion plate at any occasion. — *Cathy Jakicic*

335

1 On a head pin, string a bicone crystal and a spacer. Make the first half of a wrapped loop (Basics, p. 6). Make a total of eight crystal units.

2 Cut a 3-in. (7.6 cm) piece of chain. Attach the crystal units to the bottom links, completing the wraps as you go.

Supply List

Porcelain heart beads from Clay River Designs, clayriverdesigns.com. All other porcelain components from Fire Mountain Gems and Beads, firemountaingems.com.

- **2** 22 mm porcelain-shard pendants
- **16** 4 mm round or bicone crystals
- **16** 2 mm round spacers
- **6** in. (15 cm) chain, 2–3 mm links

- **16** 1½-in. (3.8 cm) head pins
- **2** 7 mm jump rings
- pair of earring wires
- chainnose pliers
- roundnose pliers
- diagonal wire cutters

3 Open a jump ring (Basics). Attach a pendant to the other end of the chain. Close the jump ring.

4 Open the loop of an earring wire (Basics). Attach a link so the pendant hangs lower than the crystals. Close the loop. Make a second earring.

336-341

← Linked snowballs

← Tubes on fine chain

← Snowballs and dove

← Asymmetrical hearts

← An earthy look

← Two-loop pendant

Turquoise

Turquoise is the traditional December birthstone, but you can enjoy its appeal year-round. Nuggets rock huge hoops, while a single bead is charming in demure flower earrings. Glass beads also make convincing knockoffs — try faceted rounds or rondelles. *— Naomi Fujimoto*

342

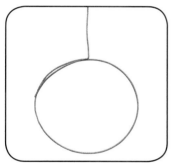

1 Cut an 8–10-in. (20–25 cm) piece of wire. Wrap it around an aspirin bottle or small juice glass. To make a stem, make a right-angle bend 1½ in. (3.8 cm) from one end.

2 String three nugget beads. Wrap the wire around the stem as in a wrapped loop (Basics, p. 6). Make a wrapped loop above the wraps.

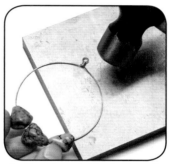

3 On a bench block or anvil, hammer the wire gently. Flip the hoop over and hammer the other side.

4 Open the loop of an earring wire (Basics). Attach the dangle and close the loop. Make a second earring to match the first.

343-348

← With decorative brass finding (Metalliferous, metalliferous.com)

← Rondelles on silver finding

← Czech glass beads on chain

← Cabochon glued to bail

← Faceted round bead on flower finding (Chelsea's Beads, chelseasbeads.com)

← Round and drop beads with open-center square

Supply List

- **6** 10–15 mm turquoise nugget beads
- 16–20 in. (41–51 cm) 20-gauge half-hard wire
- pair of earring wires
- chainnose pliers
- roundnose pliers
- diagonal wire cutters
- bench block or anvil
- hammer

Rack 'em up

To create these unusual beads, Gary Wilson (garywilsonstones.com) slices, drills, and polishes vintage billiard balls. Because the beads are so thin, they won't weigh down your lobes. You can combine the muted colors with gemstones, or try a heart or an 8-ball for old-school style. — *Naomi Fujimoto*

349

1 Cut a 4-in. (10 cm) piece of wire. Using the largest part of your roundnose pliers, make the first half of a wrapped loop (Basics, p. 6) on one end. Attach a billiard-ball slice and complete the wraps.

2 String a spacer, an accent bead, and a spacer. Make a wrapped loop perpendicular to the first loop.

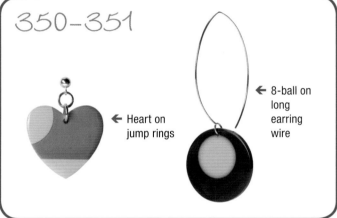

350-351

← Heart on jump rings

← 8-ball on long earring wire

3 Open the loop of an earring wire (Basics). Attach the dangle and close the loop. Make a second earring to match the first.

Supply List

- **2** 25–35 mm billiard-ball slices
- **2** 8–10 mm accent beads
- **4** 3–4 mm round spacers
- 8 in. (20 cm) 22- or 24-gauge half-hard wire
- pair of earring wires
- chainnose piers
- roundnose pliers
- diagonal wire cutters

Glassy lady

Available in virtually any shape and color, glass beads are an economical alternative to crystal. Pressed Czech glass beads lend a contemporary look to hoop earrings, while fire-polished crystals accent pre-made earring findings. If you like precise shapes, try Japanese fringe beads clustered on a hoop. — *Naomi Fujimoto*

352

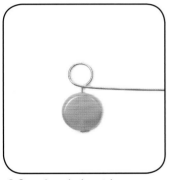

1 On a head pin, string a bead. Using the largest part of your roundnose pliers, make the first half of a wrapped loop (Basics, p. 6).

2 Attach a donut spacer and complete the wraps.

3 String the dangle on a hoop earring. About ¼ in. (6 mm) from the end of the hoop, make a right-angle bend. Make a second earring to match the first.

Supply List

- **2** 7–10 mm Czech glass beads
- **2** 10–14 mm donut spacers
- **2** 2-in. (5 cm) head pins
- pair of 20–25 mm hoop earrings
- chainnose pliers
- roundnose pliers
- diagonal wire cutters

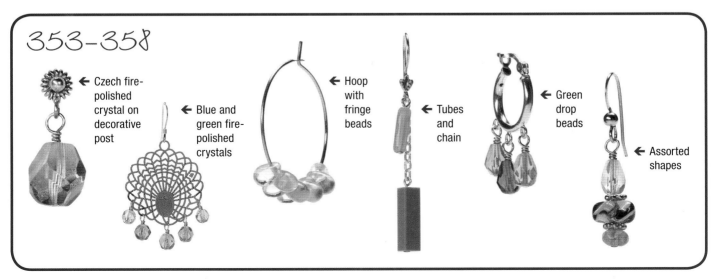

353-358

← Czech fire-polished crystal on decorative post

← Blue and green fire-polished crystals

← Hoop with fringe beads

← Tubes and chain

← Green drop beads

← Assorted shapes

Gold rush

Make opulent earrings using beads with a variety of gold finishes: shiny vermeil, brushed gold, and fire-polished crystals look precious. Even pyrite nuggets — fool's gold — are a wise choice. — *Naomi Fujimoto*

359

1 Cut a 1¼-in. (3.2 cm) piece of wire. Make a plain loop (Basics, p. 6) on one end. String an accent bead and make a plain loop. On a head pin, string a nugget bead and make a plain loop.

2 Open each loop (Basics) of the accent-bead unit. Attach the nugget unit to one loop and close the loop. Attach the dangle to an earring wire and close the loop. Make a second earring to match the first.

Supply List

- **2** 10–15 mm pyrite nugget beads (Planet Bead, planetbead.com)
- **2** 6–8 mm gold accent beads
- 2½ in. (6.4 cm) 22-gauge half-hard wire
- **2** 1½-in. (3.8 cm) 22-gauge head pins
- pair of earring wires
- chainnose pliers
- roundnose pliers
- diagonal wire cutters

360-365

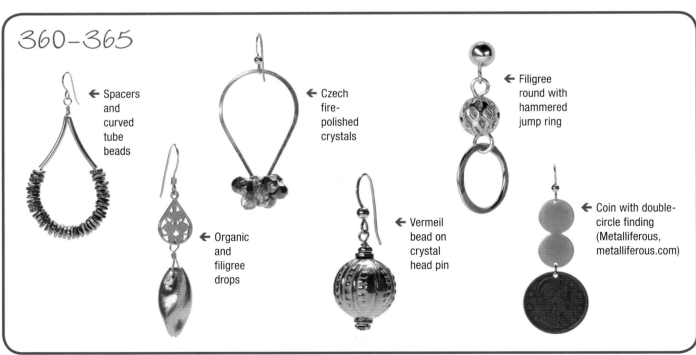

← Spacers and curved tube beads

← Czech fire-polished crystals

← Filigree round with hammered jump ring

← Organic and filigree drops

← Vermeil bead on crystal head pin

← Coin with double-circle finding (Metalliferous, metalliferous.com)

Contributors

Heather Boardman is a glass artist and jewelry designer whose work includes bright, fun colors and interesting shapes. Contact her via e-mail at heather@hmbstudios.com, or visit her Web site, hmbstudios.etsy.com.

Julie D'Amico-Beres enjoys many types of crafts in her spare time, but found her passion in beading about five years ago. She travels extensively with her husband and enjoys hunting for beads in exotic locales. Contact Julie at 262.255.4740, via e-mail at northwestbeaders@sbcglobal.net, or visit her Web site, northwestbeads.com.

Anna Elizabeth Draeger is Associate Editor of *Bead&Button* magazine. Contact her via e-mail at adraeger@beadandbutton.com, or visit her web site, web.mac.com/beadbiz.

Naomi Fujimoto is Senior Editor of *BeadStyle* magazine and the author of *Cool Jewels: Beading Projects for Teens*. Visit her blog, cooljewelsnaomi.blogspot.com, or contact her via e-mail at nfujimoto@beadstyle.com.

Sue Godfrey is a part-time jewelry artist who lives in Waukesha, Wis., with her husband and two kids. She is also an instructor for Midwest Beads in Brookfield, Wis. Contact her via e-mail at sggodfrey@wi.rr.com.

Award-winning mixed-media jewelry designer and teacher **Monica Han** lives in Potomac, Md. Contact her via e-mail at mhan@dreambeads.biz.

Linda Arline Hartung is an avid jewelry designer and teacher. Her designs and techniques are featured in many beading and jewelry-making publications around the world. Contact her via e-mail at linda@alacarteclasps.com, or visit her Web sites, alacarteclasps.com or wirelace.com.

Cathy Jakicic is Editor of *BeadStyle* magazine and the author of the book *Hip Handmade Memory Jewelry*. She has been creating jewelry for more than 15 years. Contact her via e-mail at cjakicic@beadstyle.com.

Melinda Jernigan is a full-time beaded jewelry artist from Muskogee, Okla., who specializes in one-of-a-kind boutique style jewelry. Contact her via e-mail at contact@mpdesignsjewelry.com, or visit her Web site, mpdesignsjewelry.com.

Jane Konkel is Associate Editor of *BeadStyle*, and contributed several new designs to the book *Bead Journey*. Contact her via e-mail at jkonkel@beadstyle.com.

Alice Lauber began her beading career by exhibiting her jewelry designs at art shows throughout the Midwest. In recent years, her efforts have been concentrated on running Midwest Beads, which she opened in 1997 with her husband Gary, and raising four young children. Any spare time that can be squeezed out is spent coming up with new jewelry designs. Contact Alice via e-mail at midwestbeads@sbcglobal.net.

Irina Miech is an artist, teacher, and the author of *Metal Clay for Beaders*, *More Metal Clay for Beaders*, *Inventive Metal Clay*, *Beautiful Wire Jewelry for Beaders*, and the forthcoming *Metal Clay Rings*. She also oversees Eclectica, a 6,000-square-foot retail bead supply business and classroom studio, where she teaches classes in beading, wirework, and metal clay. Contact Irina at Eclectica, 262.641.0910, or via e-mail at eclecticainfo@sbcglobal.net.

Formerly Editorial Associate of *BeadStyle*, **Lindsay Mikulsky** is currently pursuing a career in education. Contact her at lindsayrose5@gmail.com.

Polymer clay bead artist **Heather Powers** is the creative force behind *Bead Cruise*, *Bead Week*, and the *Art Bead Scene*. Visit her Web site, humblebeads.com, for more information or to contact her.

Salena Safranski feels most creative when she's listening to old jazz and drinking a cup of coffee. Contact Salena in care of Kalmbach Books.

Karla Schafer is a full-time designer at Auntie's Beads and now leads the Karla Kam program, free online instructional beading videos. Contact Karla via e-mail at karla@auntiesbeads.com, or visit her Web site, auntiebeads.com.

Sara Strauss was trained in jewelry design at the Fashion Institute of Technology in New York. Contact her via e-mail at bluestaro@hotmail.com, or visit her Web sites, sgsjewelry.com and sgsjewelry.etsy.com.

Amy Thompson creates her modern and handmade items in Cincinnati, Ohio. Contact her via e-mail at jewelrybybutterfly@yahoo.com, or visit her Web site, butterflyjewelry.etsy.com.

Contact **Stacie Thompson** in care of Kalmbach Books.

Making your own jewelry can be fast, easy, and rewarding

Step-by-step photos and instructions make more than 40 projects easy to complete, while detailed supply lists simplify shopping, making beading easier than ever. Whether you have an hour, or just fifteen minutes to put together a last-minute gift or accessory, *Jewelry in a Flash* will ensure that you have enough time to create beautiful pieces.

62687 • $19.95

Available at your favorite bead or craft shop!

Order online at
www.KalmbachBooks.com
or call
1-800-533-6644
Monday – Friday, 8:30 a.m. – 4:30 p.m. Central Standard Time.
Outside the United States and Canada call 262-796-8776, ext. 661.

Create 38 beautiful birthstone projects with step-by-step photo instructions, gemstone choices—traditional or alternate, and a few basic techniques.
62557 • $21.95

Each face shape or neckline project includes step-by-step photo instructions for a necklace and a pair of earrings that go well with you and what you're wearing.
62618 • $19.95

This book explores using nature, the color wheel, art, and fabric for color inspiration in 27 unique projects from *Beading Basics: Color*. Also includes six all-new designs.
62465 • $19.95